THE *Hope* OF *Salvation*

THE *Hope* OF *Salvation*

HARDING HEDGPETH

The Hope of Salvation
Copyright © 2020 by Harding Hedgpeth. All rights reserved.

No part of this publication may be reproduced, stored in a retrieval system or transmitted in any way by any means, electronic, mechanical, photocopy, recording or otherwise without the prior permission of the author except as provided by USA copyright law.

Unless otherwise indicated, Bible quotations are taken from *The New American Standard Bible* (NASB) Version. Copyright © 1960, 1962, 1963, 1968, 1971, 1972, 1973, 1975, 1977 by the Lockman Foundation, used by permission.

Printed in the United States of America

ISBN: 978-1-64640-081-2 *Paperback*
       978-1-64640-082-9 Hardback
       978-1-64640-083-6 eBook

Library of Congress Control Number: 2019909184

1. Religion
2. Spirituality and New Age
19.04.07

TABLE OF CONTENTS

Introduction 7

Section I   Definitions 11
     Salvation 12
     Eternal Life 14
     Faith 16
     Hope 19
     Election 20

Section II   The Argument 23
     God's Perspective Vs. Man's Perspective 25
     The Pathway To Salvation 27
         Who Is Jesus? 29
         How Important Is The Bible 45
         Trusting Jesus 52
             Repentance 52
             Faith 57
             Living Right 62
             Love 68

  The Church 77
  The Paths Away From Salvation 81
    The Ways To Destruction 83
    Falling From Grace 87
    Those Who Appear To Be Saved 91
    We Cannot Know For
    Certain We Will Be Saved 95
    The Danger Of Assurance
    Teaching 98
    Deception 101

  God's Elect 111
    Characteristics Of God's Elect 113
    Bearing Fruit 116

  The Assurance Passages 118
  The Hopeful Passages 126

Section III Why Is A Hopeful Mindset So
      Important? 131

  The Need For Perseverance 132
  It Is Difficult To Be Saved 133
  The Great Tribulation 135
  More Dangers Of Assurance Teaching 140
  The Benefits Of A Hopeful Mindset 144

Section IV How Then Shall We Live 151

Conclusion 165

INTRODUCTION

What happens to us after we die? It is an age-old question. If you were to poll a sample of people from around the world, the answer to this question would vary wildly. Some believe that this life is all there is. When we die we simply cease to exist. Others believe that we are reincarnated into another person. The Judeo-Christian view is that there is a God. There is also a heaven and a hell. After we die we will spend eternity in one of those two places. The preferred location is heaven. We in the Judeo-Christian community hope we will make it to heaven. We have a 'hope for salvation.' In this book I will focus on the Christian worldview, because it is a view that I share.

Just as there is diversity in beliefs among the world's people, there is diversity of beliefs within the Christian community. A better way to state it is that there is confusion in Christianity. A poll of Americans would reveal that most profess to be Christian. However there is radical variation among people as to what it means to be a Christian. There is not a shared mental image when the word, Christian, is used. In this book I want to examine one such variation in viewpoint and teaching. That is the viewpoint that one can know for certain that one will make it to heaven.

Many Christian organizations teach 'assurance of salvation' to their congregations. In other words, they teach that salvation is gained through a profession of faith in Jesus Christ; and once gained cannot be lost. They teach that at the moment the willing heart accepts Jesus, that person gains eternal life; and eternal life cannot be lost. After all, the phrase 'eternal life' contains the word eternal—hence forever.

These words and concepts sound right, but I believe some Christian organizations are setting their people up for a big fall with this teaching. Eternal life as defined in the Bible does not necessarily equal salvation while a person is alive. As I will demonstrate, a person can have and lose 'eternal life' through personal choices.

In this book I will illustrate that the Bible teaches that God has predestined some for salvation. They are called His elect. God knows who these people are; but mankind does not. I will further illustrate that even God's elect do not know for certain that they are God's elect. The best they can do is hope they are and persevere in righteousness (right living) until the end of their lives. Only after they die will they know for certain that they are one of God's elect. Indeed the Bible teaches that they have an 'assurance of hope,' but it does not teach that they have an 'assurance of salvation.'

In this book I will differentiate between two mindsets. One mindset will be the **'assurance'** mindset. This is the popular mindset taught by many churches and evangelists today. This is the notion that one can know with full assurance that one has salvation and nothing or no one (including one's self) can take it away. The other mindset I will call the **'hopeful'** mindset. This is a mindset that says 'I think I am one of God's elect, because I have a strong desire to trust and obey the Lord Jesus Christ. I will persevere to the end of my life in trusting and obeying God, and will remain hopeful that I will be saved.'

Why do I think it is important to have a **'hopeful'** versus **'assurance'** mindset? Because with the **'assurance'** mindset there is a diminished motivation to persevere in the faith; especially when the going gets tough. In the book of Revelation we see judgment coming to the earth and the appearance of a person characterized as 'the beast.' 'The beast' will require people to worship him and evidence their worship by putting a 'mark' on their forehead or hand. Any person refusing will not be able to buy or sell anything. A professed Christian with the **'assurance'** mindset may obey 'the beast' thinking his or her salvation cannot be lost, no matter what. That person would be condemned to spend an eternity in hell. On the other hand, a believer with a **'hopeful'** mindset would refuse 'the beast' and suffer whatever consequences resulted from being faithful to Jesus Christ. This person would persevere in following the Word of God. This would be in accordance with Scripture that says we must persevere to the end to be saved. (Matthew 24:13)

This book will be divided into four sections. I will devote the first section of this book to definitions. I do this because while we may use the same words in defining our beliefs, we have different mental images when we use those words. In other words we don't communicate our thoughts very well. I think it is vitally important that we have a common and more importantly a Biblically based understanding of such things as Salvation, Eternal Life, Faith, Hope and Election. Next, I will present and defend the argument that one cannot know for certain that he or she is one of God's elect. Then, I will discuss the importance of a 'hopeful' mindset. Finally, I will provide some strategies and examples on how we should live our lives as we progress on the journey toward salvation. So then, let's get on with the task.

Section I

DEFINITIONS

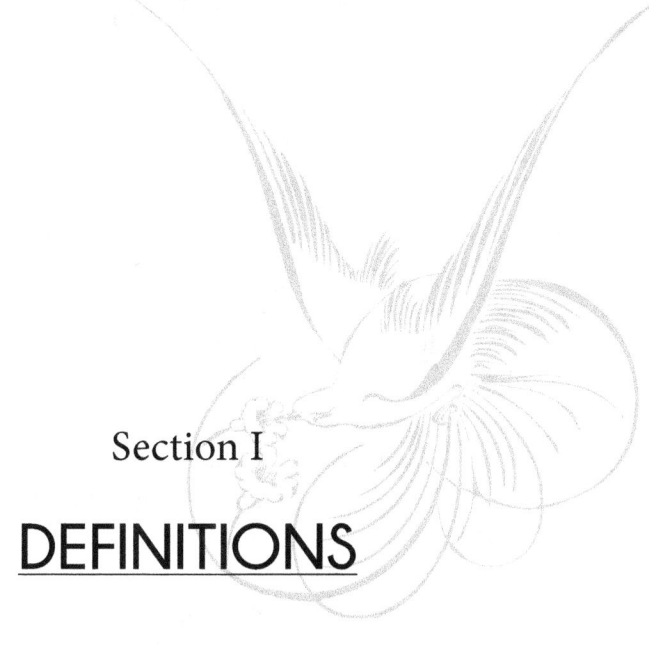

I BEGIN THIS BOOK WITH definitions because a shared mental image is vitally important when discussing such things as Salvation, Eternal Life, Faith, Hope, and Election. I believe many misconceptions are rooted in variable definitions. The proper definitions of these important concepts are found in the Bible; not in sermons or church literature. For example, let's look briefly at the term, 'eternal life.' On the surface, the meaning seems obvious. Eternal means forever and life means 'not death.' So, we reason, eternal life means living forever. But that is not how the Bible defines eternal life. Jesus defined eternal life as He prayed for his disciples in the following manner: "And this is eternal life, that they may know Thee, the only true God, and Jesus Christ whom Thou hast sent." (John 17:3) So then, the meaning of eternal life is not so simply explained. From Jesus' definition, we see that eternal life has a much deeper meaning…knowing God and Jesus

Christ. I challenge anyone to accurately characterize 'knowing God and Jesus Christ.' To gain an understanding one must probe deeper into Scripture. One thing is for certain, however. Eternal life has a present and hopefully a future value. What I want to do in this section is to look at Salvation, Eternal Life, Faith, Hope, and Election in more depth using scriptural references. Hopefully this will result in you the reader and me having that shared mental image, as these terms are frequently used throughout this book. Let's begin by looking at salvation.

Salvation

Throughout the Bible we read about salvation. In short, salvation is "being saved" from something. Noah was saved from drowning because he built the Ark. "By faith Noah, being warned by God about things not yet seen, in reverence prepared an ark for the salvation of his household, by which he condemned the world, and became an heir of the righteousness which is according to faith."(Hebrews 11:7) For the most part, though, Biblical salvation means being saved from hell, and being admitted into the Kingdom of God or heaven. Numerous Scripture passages indicate that salvation is a future event. In other words we are saved after a life well lived, not during. Salvation is not realized until one physically dies. Here are just a few of such passages:

> Matthew 10:22 "And you will be hated by all on account of My name, but **it is the one who has endured to the end** who **will** be saved."
>
> Romans 13:11 "…for now salvation is **nearer** to us than when we believed."

> Matthew 24:9-13 "Then they will deliver you to tribulation, and will kill you, and you will be hated by all nations on account of My name. And **at that time many will fall away** and will deliver up one another and hate one another. And many false prophets will arise, and will mislead many. And because lawlessness is increased, most people's love will grow cold. But **the one who endures to the end, he <u>shall be saved</u>**."
>
> Mark 13:13 "And you will be hated by all on account of My name, but **the one who endures to the end, he <u>shall be saved</u>**."

I believe salvation can be rightly characterized as the end of a journey. Scripture supports this with words and phrases such as 'being saved,' 'will be saved,' and 'leading to salvation.' In other words, as we walk the Christian walk we are being daily molded and shaped. As long as we focus on the salvation goal in thought word and deed, we will likely reach it. Although, as I will demonstrate in this book, we can never be certain that we won't at some time 'fall or jump off the track.' Some Scripture passages that support the notion that we are on a salvation journey where we are 'being saved' follow:

> Acts 2:47 "And the Lord was adding to their number day by day **those who were <u>being saved</u>**."
>
> Romans 13:11 "And this do, knowing the time, that it is already the hour for you to awaken from your sleep; **for now salvation is <u>nearer to us than when we believed</u>**."
>
> 2 Corinthians 2:15 "For we are a fragrance of Christ to God among those who are **<u>being saved</u>**…"

2 Timothy 3:15 "...the sacred writings which are able to give you the wisdom that **leads to salvation through faith which is in Christ Jesus.**"

Having seen that salvation is the hopeful end of a life's journey, let's now look at eternal life.

Eternal Life

Eternal life is defined in the Bible by Jesus as follows: "And **this is eternal life, that they may know Thee, the only true God, and Jesus Christ whom Thou hast sent.**"(John 17:3) This passage implies that when one believes in Jesus Christ, trusts Him and draws closer to Him, that person is given what is called eternal life. Their life is fuller and richer for it, and I believe they enjoy what is characterized as the fruits of the Holy Spirit: "...love, joy, peace, patience, kindness, goodness, faithfulness, gentleness, and self-control..." (Galatians 5:22-23)

Many people think that salvation and eternal life are the same things. They are not. **Eternal life has both a present and future value. Salvation has only a future value.** Eternal life can be enjoyed while a person is still physically alive. Salvation occurs after a person physically dies. I suppose one could say eternal life and salvation become equal only after a person dies.

To illustrate, let's look at physical and spiritual life and death. The Bible defines spiritual death as separation from God and spiritual life as union with God. Therefore, one can be physically alive and spiritually Dead at the same time. One can also be physically dead and spiritually alive at the same time. **This Is salvation**. This is the state of God's elect after physical death.

What about being both spiritually and physically alive? Is this salvation? I maintain that it is not. I believe that these individuals are active believers in Jesus Christ, and they enjoy the fruits of the Holy Spirit. However, their faith in Jesus is under constant scrutiny, and God is still testing them. They have yet to attain salvation. They still have the potential of turning from their faith. They can yet lose their eternal life. They have the potential of failing the tests that lie ahead. **In this state they may appear to others and even to themselves to be of God's elect.** However they cannot know for certain that they are. They must hope that they are and persevere in faith until they die physically. At that point their trials will end and they will have, as Paul put it, 'finished the race' and hear the Lord say, 'well done good and faithful servant.'

Here are some other Scripture passages that illuminate and illustrate the nature of eternal life.

> 1 John 5:11-12 "**And the witness is this, that God has given us eternal life, and this life is in His Son. He who has the Son has the life; he who does not have the Son of God does not have the life**."

> John 3:36 "**He who believes in the Son has eternal life**; but **he who does not <u>obey</u> the Son shall not see life**, but the wrath of God abides on him."

In order to gain a clearer picture of the concept of eternal life, it is helpful to think of it as a key. When we give our lives to Jesus we get the key. The key opens many wonderful things to us such as the fruits of the Holy Spirit: "…love, joy, peace, patience, kindness, goodness, faithfulness, gentleness, and self-control..." (Galatians 5:22-23) Now, if someone or something tries to take away this key, God prevents them or it. However, we have the option of throwing away the key if we so desire. But if we do not possess the key when we die, Jesus will say to us, 'Away from me, I never knew you.' (Matthew 7:23) We must persevere, therefore, in retaining the key, because there will be temptations to abandon it for the sake of something we may value more.

Hopefully we now have a shared mental image of how the Bible characterizes and defines eternal life. Let's next turn to the word, faith.

Faith

Again, I turn to Scripture for the most reliable definition. "Now faith is **the assurance of things hoped for**, the conviction of things not seen."(Hebrews 11:1) To me this means that I am certain of an outcome, an outcome that has yet to be seen. Let me provide some examples to illustrate.

When the sun sets at night, I have faith that it will rise again in the morning. It hasn't risen, yet, but I am certain that it will. Why am I so certain? Because the sun has risen every day of my life. I believe it will continue to do so, and I structure my life accordingly. I make preparations to do things that will require daylight conditions to accomplish because I know the sun will again provide the daylight. That is faith, which is based on experience.

When the winter is here, I make plans for summer vacations, because I have faith that the winter weather will change to spring and the spring to summer. I am confident because it has happened that way all the years of my life. Again, my faith is based on experience.

If I want to go clam digging at the beach, I will want to do so at low tide, so I plan according to the tide tables which tell me when low tide will occur. I leave my house to arrive at the beach at a certain time to allow me to dig at low tide. I have confidence that low tide will occur at the time indicated in the tide tables. Again, I have faith that is based on personal experience. Faith based on experience is not too hard to possess. However there is another kind of faith that is more difficult to possess: that is faith without prior experience to indicate the outcome.

Biblical faith is faith without prior experience to indicate the outcome. When God told Noah to build an ark because God was going to destroy the world with a flood, Noah had to have faith that was not based on experience. He had to have faith in God, faith that what God said would come to pass. This was not based on experience, because there had never before been a flood on the earth. The following Biblical passage speaks of Noah's faith. "By faith Noah, being warned by God about things not yet seen, in reverence prepared an ark for the salvation of his household, by which he condemned the world, and **became an heir of the righteousness which is according to faith**."(Hebrews 11:7)

When God told Abraham to leave his home and go to a faraway land, Abraham had to have faith in God. He had to have faith that God would not lead him astray, and that God would do what He said He would do. This was not based on experience. It was a faith that was based solely on Abraham's trust in God. In the book of Romans the apostle Paul spoke of Abraham's faith as follows:

> Romans 4:20-22 "…yet, with respect to the promise of God, he did not waiver in unbelief, but grew strong in faith, giving glory to God, and being fully assured that

what He had promised, He was able also to perform. Therefore it was reckoned to him as righteousness."

This is the kind of faith that God desires of us. Following are some Biblical passages that indicate the value God places on faith:

> Hebrews 10:38 "But My righteous one shall live by faith; and if he shrinks back, My soul has no pleasure in him."
>
> Galatians 3:11 "Now, that no one is justified by the Law before God is evident; for, "The righteous man shall live by faith."
>
> Hebrews 11:6 "And without faith it is impossible to please Him, for he who comes to God must believe that He is, and that He is a rewarder of those who seek Him."

Now, while it is true that God wants his people to live by faith, in what or whom does God want us to have faith? I think the Bible is quite clear that God wants us to have faith in His Son, Jesus Christ-faith that Jesus is the Son of God and faith to trust Jesus and do what He commands of us. Later in this book I will more deeply deal with faith in Jesus, but the following statement by Paul is illustrative of the importance of this faith.

> Philippians 3:8-9 "...I count all things to be loss in view of the surpassing value of knowing Christ Jesus my Lord, for whom I have suffered the loss of all things, and count them but rubbish in order that I may gain Christ, and may be found in Him, **not having a righteousness of my own derived from the Law, but <u>that which is through faith in Christ, the righteousness which comes from God on the basis of faith</u>**."

I trust that we now share an understanding of faith, so I next turn to hope.

Hope

Simply put, hope is a desire for something to occur. There are many things we hope for in this life. We hope for good health, prosperity, a good marriage, healthy children and a joyful life to name a few. Now, here is a crucial question? Does the fact that we hope for something mean that it will occur? The obvious answer is no. You probably have heard the phrase, 'hope for the best but expect the worse.' We think that with this mindset, we will avoid unbearable disappointment if our 'hoped-for event' does not come to pass. The point here is that **hope is not assurance**. When we hope for something, we are not assured that it will happen.

The next point I want to make is we can have an impact on the outcome of some events, while other events are out of our control. For example, I can hope for good weather on the weekend, but I cannot influence what the weather will be. On The other hand, if I am a student taking an exam, my preparation can directly affect the results. My hope for an 'A' can be more likely realized if I study diligently. Biblical hope is more like the latter. In other words, my hope for salvation is more likely realized through my obedience to God. The following Biblical passages illustrate the nature of Biblical hope:

> Psalm 119:166 "I **hope** for Thy salvation, O Lord, and do Thy commandments."
>
> Romans 8:24-25 "For in hope we have been saved, but **hope that is seen is not hope**; for why does one

also hope for what he sees? But if we hope for what we do not see, with perseverance we wait eagerly for it."

Isaiah 49:23 "Those who **hopefully** wait for Me will not be put to shame."

Hebrews 3:6 "…but Christ was faithful as a Son over His house whose house we are, **if we hold fast our confidence and the boast of our hope firm until the end.**"

Hopefully (no pun intended), you and I now share an understanding of Biblical hope. Later in the book I will look more closely at this hope. Indeed, hope is the central point of this book, 'The Hope of Salvation.' **We live our lives having a hope of salvation**. We are not assured of salvation during our lifetime. We will have many trials to test our faith. As with any test, it is possible to pass. It is also possible to fail. Let's now look at the concept of election.

Election

Election in the Bible means chosen. God has chosen certain people for salvation, and He chose these people for salvation before they were even born.

Romans 8:29-30 "For **whom He foreknew, He also predestined to become conformed to the image of His Son**, that He might be the first-born among many brethren; and whom He predestined, these He also called; and whom He called, these He also justified; and whom He justified, these He also glorified."

This concept of election causes much consternation and naturally leads to the question, 'am I one of God's Elect?' The short but Biblically consistent answer is **'I don't know, but I hope I am.'** The following passage suggests that God's elect will be revealed at a later time.

> Romans 8:19 "For the anxious longing of the creation **waits eagerly for the revealing of the sons of God.**" (Creation doesn't yet know who they are.)

Later in the book, I will address the characteristics of God's elect, characteristics that seem to indicate who are His people. However as I will demonstrate, who we are at this moment may not be who we are tomorrow. We may think we are one of God's elect, but we must persevere in obeying God until the end of our lives hoping that we are. We must follow Peter's advice and counsel given in the following passage.

> 2 Peter 1:10-11 "Therefore, brethren, **be all the more diligent to make certain about His calling and choosing you**; for as long as you practice these things, you will never stumble; for in this way the entrance into the eternal kingdom of our Lord and Savior Jesus Christ will be abundantly supplied to you."

We all believe that the apostle Paul is of God's elect, but even Paul held the attitude that salvation was not a 'done deal' for him. Here's what he wrote:

> Philippians 3:11-14 "...in order that I may attain to the resurrection from the dead. **Not that I have already obtained it, or have already become perfect, but I press on** in order that I may lay hold

of that for which also I was laid hold of by Christ Jesus. Brethren,

I do not regard myself as having laid hold of it yet; but one thing I do: forgetting what lies behind and reaching forward to what lies ahead, I press on toward the goal for the prize of the upward call of God in Christ Jesus."

We have looked at Salvation, Eternal Life, Faith, Hope, and Election and hopefully have gained a shared mental image of these important concepts. We can now proceed to the argument or thesis of this book: That mankind cannot know who are God's elect. Only God knows. Mankind cannot know who will and who will not attain salvation. However, one can have a healthy and strong hope that he or she will be saved.

Section II

The Argument

MANY CHURCHES TEACH TODAY that salvation is gained in the following manner: One professes a belief in Jesus Christ, that Jesus is the only Son of God. The person repents of personal sins, i.e., the person is sorry for personal sins and desires not to sin anymore. The person then acknowledges that Jesus died for our sins, and that our sins may be forgiven through our belief in Jesus. Finally, the person trusts Jesus to help he or she to live their lives and lead them out of bondage to sin.

I would agree that these are essentials to salvation. However many churches go one step further and say that once a person believes in Jesus, he or she is saved at that moment and cannot lose that salvation. This is where I disagree. I agree that one cannot lose one's salvation, but salvation does not occur until one physically dies. I further maintain that no one can know for certain that they will gain salvation, and I mean no one…not even Billy Graham, the Pope or Mother Theresa. Only God knows who are His elect-those who will gain salvation. The **best anyone can do is live a faith-filled life and hope for their salvation**.

To support my thesis, 'one cannot know for certain if one is of God's elect,' I will present the following argument: 1.) The Bible is written from two perspectives, God's and man's. That explains seemingly contrary passages that suggest on one hand that one cannot lose one's salvation and on the other hand some have fallen away. From God's perspective, His elect cannot be lost. From man's perspective some have fallen away from 'the faith.' However they weren't the elect. 2.) I will next attempt to explain the pathway to salvation, which is exclusively through Jesus Christ. I will attempt to reveal who Jesus is from Scripture, because one must accurately characterize Jesus in order for belief to have any meaning. I will further demonstrate the importance of the Bible in one's salvation journey. 3.) The next step in the argument will be to discuss the paths that lead away from salvation, and there are many. While there is only one way to salvation, there are many paths away from it. In this section I will discuss 'falling from grace,' talk about those who appear to be of God's elect, and speak to the dangers of 'assurance teaching.' I will close this phase of the argument with a discussion about deception. 4.) The next major topic in the argument will be to talk about God's elect, specifically focusing on their characteristics. 5.) The argument would not be complete unless I address the 'assurance passages.' These are the passages that the 'assurance of salvation' teachers hang their hat on. I will deal with each and every one of them, demonstrating from Scripture that these passages do not give an assurance of salvation. 6.) I will close the argument with a discussion of what I call the 'hopeful passages.' These are the passages that tell us to be hopeful of our salvation. Nowhere does the Bible have the words, 'assurance of salvation.' However the Bible does contain the words, 'hope of salvation.' So then, let's get on with the argument.

God's Perspective vs. Man's Perspective

To begin this discussion it is fruitful to take a brief look at Calvinism and Armenianism. While I won't go into all of the tenants of each viewpoint, I will look at each camp's view of salvation. Calvinists believe that salvation for 'believers' is gained during the 'believer's' lifetime. They further believe that it (salvation) cannot be lost, no matter what happens in the 'believer's' lifetime. Armenianism, on the other hand, teaches that salvation can be gained and it can also be lost in a 'believer's' lifetime. Armenians believe that people can be saved, but as a consequence of their poor choices they can lose their salvation. The interesting point here is that the Bible contains passages that support both beliefs. Let's look at two of them. The first passage is spoken by Jesus and is taken from the book of John.

> John 6:37 "All that the Father gives Me shall come to Me, and **the one who comes to Me I will certainly not cast out.**"

This is but one passage Calvinists use to illustrate that a believer cannot lose his or her salvation. However they have difficulty with this next passage, which the Armenians use to their advantage.

> Hebrews 6:4-6 "For in the case of **those who have once been enlightened and have tasted of the heavenly gift and have been made partakers of the Holy Spirit**, and have tasted the good word of God and the powers of the age to come, **and then have fallen away**, it is impossible to renew them again to repentance, since they again crucify to themselves the Son of God, and put Him to open shame."

I have heard and read many 'hand waving' distortions of this passage to try to make it not mean what it says. However, it does mean what it says. So then, how can both passages be true? The answer occurred to me suddenly one day while I was exercising. The Bible is written from two perspectives–God's and man's. God knows those who will be saved. These are the ones who will come to Jesus in a total and sincere manner. Those who do come to Jesus in that total and sincere manner will not be cast out. More importantly, they will not choose to depart from their belief. From man's perspective it appears, as in Hebrews 6:4-6, that there are some who will lose their salvation. From God's perspective, a person doesn't lose his or her salvation. They simply never had it in the first place, because they were not one of God's elect.

The fact that the Bible is written from two perspectives is wonderfully illustrated in the Psalms. Look at the first four verses of the Psalm 89 where David begins speaking in the first person; then suddenly and without warning, God is speaking:

> Psalm 89:1-4
>
> "I will sing of the loving kindness of the Lord forever;

> To all generations I will make known Thy faithfulness with my mouth.
>
> For I have said, "Lovingkindness will be built up forever;
>
> In the heavens Thou wilt establish Thy faithfulness."
>
> **"I have made a covenant with My chosen; I have sworn to David My servant, I will establish your seed forever, and build up your throne to all generations."**

Many of the Psalms have this dual perspective: Psalms 2, 22, 32, 45, 50, 75, 81, 90, 95, 108, to name a few. The book of Isaiah also contains numerous passages from God's perspective. I have also heard Bible teachers comparing the books of Kings and Chronicles and concluding that Kings is from man's perspective and Chronicles is from God's perspective. Also, have you ever considered that all of Jesus' words are from God's perspective? So when Jesus says, **"All that the Father gives Me shall come to Me,** and the one who comes to Me I will certainly not cast out," (John 6:37) He is saying that God knows who will come to Him with a sincere heart.

The Pathway to Salvation

The Bible is quite clear that the only way to salvation is through Jesus Christ. The following passage spoken by Jesus leaves no doubt in my mind.

> John 14:6 "Jesus said to him, "**I am the way, and the truth,** and **the life; no one comes to the Father, but through Me."**

The apostle Peter on the day of Pentacost further solidified that Jesus is the only way to salvation with the following passage:

> Acts 4:12 "And **there is salvation in no one else**; for there is no other name under heaven that has been given among men, by which we must be saved."

Having established this important truth, the following questions remain: What does that mean, and what do I need to do? The Bible says that I must believe in Jesus to be saved. The following passage, which answered the question of the Philippian jailer, indicates this:

> Acts 16:30-31 "…and after he brought them out, he said, "Sirs, what must I do to be saved?" And they said, "**Believe in the Lord Jesus, and you shall be saved**, you and your household."

What does that mean? The following passage from the book of Romans provides a little more guidance, but still leaves some confusion:

> Romans 10:9-10 "…if you confess with your mouth Jesus as Lord, and believe in your heart that God raised Him from the dead, you **shall** be saved; for with the heart man believes, resulting in righteousness, and with the mouth he confesses, **resulting in salvation**."

So, there still remains some confusion. What does it really mean to believe in Jesus? Further, how do we do it? More importantly, who is Jesus? **We can believe in Jesus all of our life with no benefit, if we don't accurately**

characterize Him. So, at this point we need to focus on knowing who He is before we attempt to believe in Him.

Who is Jesus?

Many in this world use the name Jesus, but they don't really know who He is. Some think He is just a great teacher, while others think He is only a prophet. There is even a professed Christian organization that thinks Jesus is the spirit brother of Satan. Another professed Christian group thinks He is one of God's created beings. So you see, there is confusion about the character of Jesus. In fact, the pivotal question that reveals any person's true belief is: 'Who do you say Jesus is?' It was a question that Jesus asked his disciples with varied responses. Let's look at that conversation.

> Matthew 16:13-17 "Now when Jesus came into the district of Caesarea Philippi, He began asking His disciples, saying, "Who do people say that the Son of Man is?" And they said, "Some say John the Baptist; and others, Elijah; but still others, Jeremiah, or one of the prophets." He said to them, "But who do you say that I am?" And Simon Peter answered and said, "**Thou art the Christ, the Son of the living God**." And Jesus answered and said to him, "Blessed are you, Simon Barjona, because flesh and blood did not reveal this to you, but My Father who is in heaven."

By Jesus' response I conclude that Peter answered Jesus' question correctly. But is that all we need to know about Jesus, that He is the Son of God? Is our mere intellectual assent of this fact sufficient for our salvation? The short answer is 'no, it isn't.' Satan and his demons know that Jesus is the Son of God, but that knowledge doesn't give them a ticket into heaven. The following Bible passage is revealing in this regard:

> Matthew 8:28-29 "And when He had come to the other side into the country of the Gadarenes, two men who were demon possessed met Him as they were coming out of the tombs; they were so exceedingly violent that no one could pass by that road. And behold, they cried out, saying, **"What do we have to do with You, Son of God?** Have You come here to torment us before the time?"

The demons know that Jesus is the Son of God. They also know they are headed for eternal agony, not salvation. So, we see that merely acknowledging that Jesus is the Son of God is not sufficient.

There is so much more that we need to know about the character of Jesus before we can properly believe in Him. When we have a more complete picture of Jesus we will be motivated to trust in Him to guide us and change us as we need to be changed. More importantly, we will know how to go about trusting in Him. How then can we more completely understand who Jesus is? There is only one way to understand, and that is through reading the Bible.

The Bible has much to say about Jesus and who He is. So, where do we begin? I believe a good beginning is to see what Jesus said about Himself. Following are several of what I call the 'I am' passages where Jesus provides direct clues about His nature. We'll look at each one of them separately. In the first passage, Jesus characterizes Himself as the bread of life.

Jesus, The Bread of Life

> John 6:48-51 "**I am the bread of life**. Your fathers ate the manna in the wilderness, and they died. This is the bread which comes down out of heaven, so that one may eat of it and not die. **I am the living bread that came down out of heaven**; if anyone eats of this bread, he shall live forever; and the bread also which I shall give for the life of the world is My flesh."

Jesus spoke these words in the town of Capernaum, and He lost many of His followers as a result. They couldn't understand what Jesus was saying to them. I'm sure they had mental images of cannibalism and were confused. We don't need to be confused, because we have the Bible to interpret what Jesus was saying. In order to understand what Jesus meant we have to look at the following Bible passage.

> John 1:1 "In the beginning was the Word, and the Word was with God, and the Word was God."

This passage characterizes Jesus as the Word of God. The Bible is the Word of God. We can therefore 'eat the body of Jesus' by partaking of the Bible. It then becomes for us real spiritual food, and our daily reading the Bible nourishes us spiritually. Now, I understand that our human logic is difficult to apply here. How can anybody be a book, you might think.

However if you think of the Bible as a complete description of Jesus, then **you can conceive of reading the Bible as a means of getting to know Jesus.** We are taking that knowledge into our bodies and are literally being nourished by it (the knowledge). And remember the description of eternal life? It is knowing Jesus. So, as we get to know Him, We are gaining eternal life. Let's turn to another 'I am' passage.

In the following passage Jesus characterizes Himself as light.

Jesus, The Light

> John 8:12 "…**Jesus spoke to them, saying, "I am the Light of the world**; he who follows Me shall not walk in the darkness, but shall have the light of life."

Jesus did not say that He was 'a' light of the world. Rather He said that He was 'the' light of the world. Let's look at what this means. First we agree that light illuminates, and when light illuminates we can identify and avoid hazards. From a spiritual viewpoint, Jesus reveals things that will harm us and lead us to death. He also reveals things that will lead to life. The Bible teaches that from a spiritual standpoint, this world is ruled by Satan. (Luke 4:6) Therefore it is shrouded in spiritual darkness. Jesus is the only light that will shine through this darkness. This characteristic of Jesus is further illustrated in following passage from Psalm 119 spoken by King David:

> Psalm 119:105 "Thy word is a lamp to my feet, and a light to my path."

King David knew the importance of God's Word, and he delighted in it. David did not know about Jesus at the time, but he did know where the truth existed. David characterized God's truth as light, and so it is. Recall, also, that Jesus characterized Himself as The Truth. See how it all fits together so wonderfully. Let's now look at another of Jesus' personal characterizations.

Jesus, The Way, The Truth and The Life

We have already looked briefly at the following passage, but it is so rich that it deserves more discussion.

> John 14:6 **"Jesus said to him, "I am the way, and the truth, and the life; no one comes to the Father but through Me."**

When Jesus says He is 'the way,' He means He is the only way to salvation. Early Christians were called 'followers of the way.' Frankly, I prefer this descriptor to the word Christian. It more effectively describes a true believer in Jesus Christ. True believers follow Jesus. The disciples followed Jesus, and in so doing, got to know Jesus. We follow Jesus by trying to do what He says and emulate Him. The 'what would Jesus do' phrase is a legitimate test for us when we are faced with a difficult decision. Doing what Jesus would do is an effective means to follow Jesus who is 'the way.' Again, we have to read the Bible to know what Jesus would do.

Jesus further said He is 'the truth.' Notice again, He didn't say He was 'a truth.' Rather, He said He is 'the truth.' What does this mean, and how should we apply it in our lives? Again, it is helpful to characterize Jesus as the living Word of God. It is also helpful to apply a little Algebra here. First, we need to look at the following passage from Psalm 119.

> Psalm 119:160 "The sum of Thy word is truth, and every one of Thy righteous ordinances is everlasting."

The 'sum of Thy word' in this passage is literally the entire Bible. Now, let's apply the Algebra. If Jesus (A) is the Truth (C), and if the Word of God (B) is the Truth (C), then it follows that Jesus (A) is the Word of God (B). Once Again we see that the entire Bible Characterizes Jesus. We therefore apply this knowledge in our lives by reading and studying the Bible. Do you see how important the Bible is to our journey of faith? Do you see how important the Bible is in having any meaningful belief in Jesus?

The final characterization of Jesus in John 14:6 is that He is 'the life.' What does that mean? Sometimes in order to determine what something is, it is helpful to look at what it is not. The opposite of life is death. The Bible defines spiritual death as separation from God. Therefore, spiritual life must be union or fellowship with God. Further, we have seen eternal life characterized as knowing Jesus. The following passages provide additional insight into the nature of the life that Jesus provides.

> 1 John 5:11-12 "And the witness is this, that **God has given us eternal life**, and **this life is in His Son.** He who has the Son has the life; **he who does not have the Son of God does not have the life.**"
>
> John 1:4-5 "**In Him was life**, and **the life was the light of men**. And the light shines in the darkness, and the darkness did not comprehend it."

These passages indicate that the life we need resides in Jesus. In order for us to benefit from that life we must reside with or in Jesus. Again, our human logic gets in the way. How in the world do we reside in Jesus? The answer is not physically discerned. Rather it is spiritual. We must look at all of these truths with spiritual eyes. The Bible says that if we abide in Jesus, we will bear fruit. (John 15:5) Abiding in, residing in, they are the same. Again, if Jesus is the Word of God, we can abide in Jesus by abiding in or studying the Word of God, the Bible. Wow! Is that ever an important book!

Jesus, The Door

> Jesus also characterized Himself as the 'door.' Let's look at the following passage.
>
> John 10:7-10 "Jesus therefore said to them again, "Truly, truly, I say to you, **I am the door of the sheep.** All who came before Me are thieves and robbers, but the sheep did not hear them. **I am the door; if anyone enters through Me, he shall be saved, and shall go in and out and find pasture.** The thief comes only to steal, and kill, and destroy; **I came that they may have life, and have it abundantly.**"

Jesus also spoke the following passage that is similar but raises for us a serious question.

> Matthew 7:13-14 "Enter by the narrow gate; for the gate is wide, and the way is broad that leads to destruction, and many are those who enter by it. **For the gate is small, and the way is narrow that leads to life, and few are those who find it.**"

The question is this. Is it easy or difficult to find the door or the gate that leads to salvation? The Matthew passage seems to indicate that it is difficult. In fact, very few people actually find it. So, you see, the 'easy to believe and be saved doctrine' taught in many churches is shaky at best. **I think the very key to finding the gate that leads to life is to accurately characterize Jesus**. Only when we accurately characterize Him can we find Him. And there is only one way to accurately characterize Jesus. That is through reading and studying the Bible.

Jesus, The True Vine

Let's look at another of Jesus' self-characterizations. In the following passage Jesus compares Himself to a grape vine.

> John 15:1-2 "**I am the true vine, and My Father is the vinedresser**. Every branch in Me that does not bear fruit, He takes away; and every branch that bears fruit, He prunes it, that it may bear more fruit."

Picture a grape vineyard, with the grape vines coming up out of the ground, and the branches growing out of the vines. The branches are trained along wires or strings, and the grapes grow out of the branches. This analogy is beautiful because Jesus is the vine, and we are the branches. The only way we can bear fruit in our lives is by being attached to Jesus. Apart from the vine, the grape branches cannot grow grapes. Apart from Jesus, we cannot bear fruit in our lives. Notice also that some branches in a vineyard don't have any grapes on them. Some branches may appear to be well attached, but they are not. Even so, some may appear to be 'in Jesus,' but they are not. Let's look at another passage that supports this characterization of Jesus.

John 15:4-8 "Abide in Me, and I in you. As the branch cannot bear fruit of itself, unless it abides in the vine, so neither can you, unless you abide in Me. I am the vine, you are the branches; **he who abides in Me, and I in him, he bears much fruit**; for apart from Me you can do nothing. **If anyone does not abide in Me, he is thrown away as a branch, and dries up; and they gather them, and cast them into the fire, and they are burned.** If you abide in Me, and My words abide in you, ask whatever you wish, and it shall be done for you. By this is My Father glorified, **that you bear much fruit, and so <u>prove</u> to be My disciples.**"

Once again, we are faced with the notion of abiding in Jesus. Once again, I conclude the only way to do that is to read and heed the Bible. At this point it is good to pause and reflect on how rich and how deep is the character of Jesus. Just acknowledging He is the Son of God is not sufficient to knowing Him. It is certainly necessary, but it is not sufficient. Another point to ponder is 'belief.' If we truly believe all of these characterizations of Jesus, how does that affect us? For example, if we truly believe that reading and studying and doing what the Bible says is the only way to abide in Jesus, does that compel us to do it? I maintain that if the believing doesn't lead to doing, then the believing is not genuine. It isn't the kind of believing that will lead to salvation. Having paused to reflect, let's look at another of Jesus' self-characterizations.

<u>Jesus, The Good Shepherd</u>

Jesus also called Himself the good shepherd as this next passage illustrates.

> John 10:14-15 "**I am the good shepherd; and I know My own, and My own know Me, even as the Father knows Me and I know the Father**; and I lay down My life for the sheep."

This is an intriguing passage, because many professed believers say they know Jesus and are of Jesus' flock. Let's focus on what I consider the key words in the passage, 'I know My own, and My own know me.' We may think we know Jesus, but do we really? Let's look at the following sobering passage.

> Matthew 7:21-23 "**Not everyone who says to Me, 'Lord, Lord,' will enter the kingdom of heaven; but he who does the will of My Father who is in heaven**. Many will say to Me on that day, 'Lord, Lord, did we not prophesy in Your name, and in Your name cast out demons, and in Your name perform many miracles?' And then I will declare to them, '**I never knew you; depart from Me, you who practice lawlessness**.'"

Who are these people about whom Jesus is speaking? They weren't just common folk. If they prophesied, cast out demons, and performed many miracles, they were most likely religious leaders. They were the ones who everybody, including themselves, especially themselves, assumed would gain entry into heaven. They thought they knew Jesus, but they didn't. So then, how do we get to know Jesus? I know it's getting redundant, but the only way to know Him is through reading and heeding the Bible. I further maintain that knowing Jesus is a process that we undertake and continue all of our lives. I don't think we ever get to completely know Him, but we get to know Him better and better every day. As we get to know Him, our hope for salvation grows stronger and stronger.

Let's look at the Shepherd characteristic. A shepherd guides and protects the sheep. Even so, Jesus guides and protects His followers. I believe that there will be many Satanic attempts to derail those who want to follow Jesus. I further believe that Jesus foils those attempts, as long as the person perseveres in following Jesus. Indeed, Jesus will protect His own. I believe that as a shepherd, Jesus also guides those who are His. He reveals spiritual dangers and convicts believers of sin in their lives. He fosters a continual repentant attitude in believers and frees them of bondage to sin in their lives, that they may follow Him more freely.

Jesus' Relationship With God the Father

The next, and I think most important characteristic of Jesus That I Want to address, is His Relationship to God the Father. I will say right up front that this is not an easy discussion. In fact, I will confess that I don't have a clear and distinct understanding of this most important characteristic. I don't think anybody really does. I think this is another area where God gives us more and more understanding, as our faith in Him grows. However I don't think we will in this lifetime be allowed to see this truth clearly.

As I researched this important characteristic, it seemed to me that Jesus' relationship with God the Father can be subdivided into two characteristics. Jesus is first the Son of God. In this capacity He is both separate and distinct from God the Father. He is also in complete unity with God the Father. Also, in this capacity He is subject to and of lower rank than God the Father. The human mind can somewhat grasp the notion of Jesus Being the Son Of God. However the second characteristic produces difficulties in understanding.

Jesus is also characterized as God the Son. Jesus is in complete unity with God the Father and is Himself characterized as God. In this capacity Jesus is so powerful that He created all things and today holds the entire universe together. Wow! Let's look at Jesus' relationship with God the Father in light of Scripture.

Jesus, The Son of God

As the Son of God, Jesus is separate and distinct from God the Father. He is also in complete unity with God the Father. Let's first look at some verses that characterize Jesus as separate and distinct from God the Father.

> John 17:3 "And this is eternal life, **that they may know Thee, the only true God, and Jesus Christ whom Thou hast sent.**"
>
> 1 John 4:14 "And we have beheld and bear witness that **the Father has sent the Son to be the Savior of the world.**"
>
> Matthew 3:17 "...and behold, a voice out of the heavens, saying, **"This is My beloved Son, in whom I am well-pleased."**

In addition to being separate and distinct from God the Father, Jesus is also characterized as being subject to God the Father. In other words, God the Father is of higher rank than Jesus. Jesus Himself indicated this as he spoke the following passages:

John 5:30 "**I can do nothing on My own initiative.** As I hear, I judge; and My judgment is just, because **I do not seek My own will, but the will of Him who sent Me.**"

John 14:28 "You heard that I said to you, 'I go away, and I will come to you.' If you loved Me, **you would have rejoiced, because I go to the Father; for the Father is greater than I.**"

John 20:17 "Jesus said to her, "Stop clinging to Me, for I have not yet ascended to the Father; but go to My brethren, and say to them, "**I ascend to My Father and your Father, and My God and your God.**"

There are many other verses that demonstrate Jesus being subject God the Father. However in addition to being separate, distinct and subject to God the Father, Jesus, the Son of God, is also in complete unity with God the Father. Now, we are starting to depart from human reason and understanding; but let's look at a couple of verses that demonstrate this unity.

John 10:30 "**I and the Father are one.**"

(Jesus speaking to the Jews in Jerusalem)

John 14:9-11 "Jesus said to him, "Have I been so long with you, and yet you have not come to know Me, Philip? **He who has seen Me has seen the Father**; how do you say, 'Show us the Father?' Do you not believe **that I am in the Father, and the Father is in Me? The words that I say to you I do not speak on My own initiative, but the Father abiding in Me does His works. Believe Me that I am in the Father, and the Father in Me;** otherwise believe on account of the works themselves."

From these verses we can see that Jesus is in complete unity with God the Father and is empowered by God to do great things. However the Bible also tells us that Jesus is deity; that He is God, also. Now we have really departed from human reasoning and understanding.

Jesus, God The Son

Have you ever heard of the word, 'Godhead?' It is not a word found in the Bible, but it serves to help us to understand the concept of Jesus being God and God the Father being God. Both Jesus and God the Father are within this Godhead. The Holy Spirit of God is also there, but I will not discuss the Holy Spirit at this point. But for the sake of this discussion, it is helpful to think of one 'what' and three 'who's.' The Godhead is the 'what;' and God the Father, Jesus and the Holy Spirit are the three 'who's' within the Godhead. God the Father, Jesus and the Holy Spirit exist together and are in unity within the Godhead. The Bible has ample evidence for this relationship; but I will focus on Jesus' position within this Godhead, and demonstrate from Scripture that He is indeed God the Son.

> John 1:1-5 "In the beginning was the Word, and the **Word was with God**, and the Word was God. He was in the beginning with God. **All things came into being by Him**, and apart from Him nothing came into being that has not come into being. In Him was life, and the life was the light of men. And the light shines in the darkness, and the darkness did not comprehend it."

The beginning of the book of John says it all. Jesus existed with God from the beginning. He was with God, and He was God. As I mentioned before, Jesus was also involved with the creation of all things, as is further evidenced by the following verse.

> Colossians 1:16-17 "**For by Him all things were created**, both in the heavens and on earth, visible and invisible, whether thrones or dominions or rulers or authorities-**all things have been created by Him and for Him**. And He is before all things, and **in Him all things hold together**."

That's pretty incredible, to think that Jesus created all things and today holds this universe together. To think of Him only as the Son of God doesn't do Him justice. The next verse is astounding in its content, as God the Father refers to Jesus as God.

> Hebrews 1:8 "But of His Son He says, "Thy throne, **O God**, is forever and ever...""

This mystery is mind-boggling and difficult to grasp. I think it best just to accept it and pray for further understanding. Let's look at other passages that indicate that Jesus is God. In the following verse, Thomas, one of Jesus' disciples, acknowledges Jesus as God in Jesus' presence. Jesus does not correct him.

> John 20:28-29 "**Thomas answered and said to Him, "My Lord and My God!"** Jesus said to him, "Because you have seen Me, have you believed? Blessed are they who did not see, and yet believed."

The apostle Paul further confirms Jesus' Diety by the following verse.

> Colossians 2:9 "For in Him all the fullness of Diety dwells in bodily form..."

So, we see that Jesus is the Son of God, separate And distinct from God. He Is also subject to and obedient to God, Receiving direction and commands from God; but He is in complete unity with God. Finally, He is God the Son, having the powers of God. How are we to understand these truths? I think this next passage will be helpful.

> Philippians 2:5-11 "Have this attitude in yourselves which was also in Christ Jesus, who, **although He existed in the form of God, did not regard equality with God a thing to be grasped,** but emptied Himself, taking the form of a bond-servant, and being made in the likeness of men. And being found in appearance as a man, He humbled Himself by becoming obedient to the point of death, even death on a cross. Therefore also **God highly exalted Him, and bestowed on Him the name which is above every name, that at the name of Jesus every knee should bow, of those who are in heaven, and on earth, and under the earth, and that every tongue should confess that Jesus Christ is Lord, to the glory of God the Father.**"

I think it is clear that God the Father is all powerful. The power of Diety comes from Him, and He bestows it on whom He pleases. Scripture indicates that Jesus existed with God the Father as Diety before He came to the earth in the form of a man. Jesus was acting on behalf of God the Father here on earth. Jesus said over and over that He said and/or did nothing on His own initiative, but said and did only as the Father commanded Him. Scripture also refers to Jesus as God's servant while He was here on earth, and Jesus acted in obedience to God. Because of Jesus' obedience, becoming the perfect sacrifice for our sins, God has bestowed on Him even more glory and power.

Jesus has become our Lord. It is to Him that we look for direction and guidance in our lives. God the Father still exists. He is still of higher rank than Jesus. However **we glorify God the Father by being obedient to His Son, Jesus.** How do we do that? Jesus is characterized as the Word of God. Therefore, we obey Him by reading the Bible and conforming our lives to what is commanded therein. The Bible is really important to our salvation.

Are you starting to become awed with Jesus? I'm certainly impressed with Him. As I said before, a simple acknowledgement that He is the Son of God is not sufficient for our salvation. There is so much more to know about Jesus. I think we can study about Him all of our lives and still only barely scratch the surface of who He is. In addition to the characteristics that I Have addressed, Jesus Is also characterized as the Lamb of God, The Teacher and the High Priest. I will leave it to you to search the Bible and understand what you can about these and other traits. We will next discuss the importance of the Bible to our salvation journey.

How Important is The Bible

In the process of trying to characterize Jesus we have seen a common thread. That common thread is the Bible.

We have seen that we cannot know who Jesus is without consulting the Bible. Therefore, it is obvious that the Bible is very important to our salvation journey. In fact, one could rightly conclude that the Bible is essential. Let's look at what the Bible has to say about itself. To start the discussion, let's look at a passage from a letter that Paul wrote to his friend, Timothy.

> 2 Timothy 3:15-17 "…from childhood you have known **the sacred writings which are able to give you the wisdom that leads to salvation through faith which is in Christ Jesus. All Scripture is inspired by God and profitable for teaching, for reproof, for correction, for training in righteousness**; that the man of God may be adequate, equipped for every good work."

The first sentence seems to indicate that reading Scripture gives a person wisdom that helps one to have faith in Jesus Christ, and that faith leads to salvation. I maintain that this wisdom can only be obtained from reading the Bible. It doesn't come from anything the world has to offer, including religion.

The Bible also says that the 'fear of the Lord is the beginning of wisdom…'(Psalm 111:10) Fearing or respecting God is the initial motivation that leads us to want to obey God. That initial step eventually leads one to read the Bible. Then, in addition to having fear or respect for God, we get to know who He is and cultivate a genuine love for Him.

The second sentence in the 2 Timothy passage indicates that all Scripture is inspired by God and is useful for many things, including training in righteousness. Righteousness is linked to faith, which is essential to salvation, as indicated in the following passages: "But the righteous man shall live by faith."(Romans 1:17) "And without faith it is impossible to please Him…" (Hebrews 11:6) We cannot know these essential truths without reading the Bible.

The Bible also helps us to fight the spiritual battles that come our way. The apostle Paul mentioned that our most important battles are not physical. Rather, they are against spiritual forces. To combat these forces we must be properly armed as the following passage indicates.

> Ephesians 6:10-18 "Finally, be strong in the Lord, and in the strength of His might. Put on the full armor of God, that you may be able to stand firm against the schemes of the devil. For our struggle is not against flesh and blood, but against the rulers, against the powers, against the world forces of this darkness, against the spiritual forces of wickedness in the heavenly places. Therefore, take up the full armor of God, that you may be able to resist in the evil day, and having done everything, to stand firm. Stand firm therefore, having girded your loins with truth, and having put on the breastplate of righteousness, and having shod your feet with the preparation of the gospel of peace; in addition to all, taking up the shield of faith with which you will be able to extinguish all the flaming missiles of the evil one. And take the helmet of salvation, and the sword of the Spirit, which is the word of God. With all prayer and petition pray at all times in the Spirit, and with this in view, be on the alert with all perseverance…"

Notice that the Bible or the Word of God is represented Twice in the 'full Armor of God.' It is first 'the Belt of truth,' and secondly it is the 'sword of the Spirit.' The Bible serves both a defensive and an offensive purpose. In fact the Word of God is the only effective means to fight against evil. King David, in the following Psalm, agreed.

> Psalm 119:11 "Thy Word I have treasured in my heart, that I may not sin against Thee."

Fighting against sin in our lives is largely a spiritual battle. It is only waged effectively by fighting it in the thought stage, and the following Bible Passage is most helpful in that regard.

> 2 Corinthians 10:5 "We are destroying speculations and every lofty thing raised up against the knowledge of God, and we are taking every thought captive to the obedience of Christ..."

I have found in my own life that when I am tempted to sin, the following prayer is most effective: 'Dear Lord, please help me to take captive my every thought for Jesus Christ that I may not sin against you.' I wouldn't have known about that effective defense if the Bible hadn't revealed it to me. The Bible is helpful in so many ways.

Jesus said that keeping His word is evidence that we love Him, as indicated in the following passage:

> John 14:23 "Jesus answered and said to him, "**If anyone loves Me, he will keep My word**; and My Father will love him, and We will come to him, and make Our abode with him."

Remember the passage about the people that Jesus told to depart because He never knew them? Those people obviously didn't know or love Jesus. The formula to draw near to Jesus is clear in the above passage. Keep Jesus' Word. How can anyone possibly do that without reading the Bible? Further, we must do what the Bible tells us to do. In so doing there will be great benefit, both now and eternally, as the following passages reveal.

> Psalm 119:165 "Those who love Thy law have great peace, and **nothing causes them to stumble.**"
>
> Psalm 19:7-11 "The **law of the Lord is perfect, restoring the soul**; the testimony of the Lord is sure, making wise the simple. The precepts of the Lord are right, rejoicing the heart; the commandment of the Lord is pure, enlightening the eyes. The fear of the Lord is clean, enduring forever; the judgments of the Lord are true; they are righteous altogether. They are more desirable than gold, yes, than much fine gold; sweeter also than honey and the drippings of the honeycomb. Moreover, **by them Thy servant is warned; in keeping them there is great reward.**"

So then, how do we go about 'keeping God's Word?' As the following passage reveals, it isn't done in one sitting with an open Bible.

> Romans 12:1-2 "…present your bodies a living and holy sacrifice, acceptable to God, which is your spiritual service of worship. And **do not be conformed to this world, but be transformed by the renewing of your mind, that you may prove what the will of God is, that which is good and acceptable and perfect.**'

As this passage indicates, it is a transformation process, through which our minds are renewed. Daily Bible reading and Bible study effects our minds. Our thoughts start to change from worldly to spiritual things. Our decisions begin to be influenced by what the Bible commands of us. Moreover, our thoughts, words and actions begin to change, because our thoughts directly affect what we say and do. We don't use course language as much. We don't lie as much. We begin to focus more on the welfare of others rather than on ourselves. We don't lust after those who are not our spouses as much. We don't gossip as much. Notice, I didn't say we stop thinking, saying and doing these things. The frequency of their occurrences begins to diminish. More importantly, we feel badly about thinking, saying or doing things that the Bible tells us not to do.

As we immerse ourselves in reading and heeding the Bible, we certainly notice a distinct behavioral change. We also reap some real benefits. These are characterized as the fruits of the Holy Spirit, as indicated in the following passage.

> Galatians 5:22-23 "But the fruit of the Spirit is love, joy, peace, patience, kindness, goodness, faithfulness, gentleness, self-control…"

The 'fruits of the Holy Spirit' is a list of personal characteristics that result from continual immersion in and obedience to the Word of God. These are real and tangible benefits from following Jesus Christ by reading and heeding the Bible. Our lives change. We begin to understand what love is, and we practice it more. We have joy without external stimulation. We have a peace that transcends all understanding, even in challenging times. We are more patient and experience less anxiety with our lives. We find ourselves being kind to people who need it. Our friends and relatives begin to characterize us as 'good' people. Our faith grows. We are gentler and less contentious in our relationships with others. We have more self-control to avoiding sinning. The Net result is an increasingly full and rich existence.

In addition to spiritual benefits there are also physical benefits to reading and heeding the Bible. The person who sincerely strives to do what the Lord commands of him prospers in virtually everything he or she undertakes, as the following passage tells us.

> Psalm 1:1-3 "How blessed is the man who does not walk in the counsel of the wicked, nor stand in the path of sinners...But **his delight is in the law of the Lord, and in His law he meditates day and night**, and he will be like a tree firmly planted by streams of water, which yields its fruit in its season, and its leaf does not wither; and **in whatever he does, he prospers**."

So, we see the benefits or blessings that we receive through reading the Bible and striving to change our lives accordingly. We also see how reading the Bible enables us to change for the better. We see that the Bible is the only way to get to know God and to accurately characterize Jesus. But there is another extremely important function that the Bible serves. It keeps us from being deceived by Satan and his followers.

Deception is a powerful tool used by Satan. Deception can lead us down paths to destruction. In fact, deception can lead us straight to hell. And guess what. If that happens to us, we have no excuse, because we have the Bible to guide us into all truth. The Bible is the only defense we have against deception. Let's look at the following sobering passage.

> 2 Thessalonians 2:8-12 "And then that lawless one will be revealed whom the Lord will slay with the breath of His mouth and bring to an end by the appearance of His coming; that is, the one whose coming is in accord with the activity of Satan, with all power and signs and false wonders, and with all the deception of wickedness for **those who perish, because they did not receive the <u>love of the truth</u> so as to be saved**. And for this reason God will send upon them a deluding influence so that they might believe what is false, in order that they all may be judged who did not believe the truth, but took pleasure in wickedness."

As this passage indicates, God will allow deception to occur in order to separate true believers from the others. **God's Judgment will be right, because it is the individual who will choose the path of deception or the path of truth.** God won't force anyone down either path.

At this point we should see that the Word of God or the Bible is an essential part of our salvation journey. Now that we more rightly characterize Jesus and understand that the Bible is essential and integral to that characterization, we are better able to discuss what it means to trust Jesus.

<u>Trusting Jesus</u>

Repentance

Recall the following formula for salvation from the book of Romans.

> Romans 10:9-10 "…if you **confess with your mouth Jesus as Lord, and believe in your heart**

> **that God raised Him from the dead**, you shall be saved; for with the heart man believes, resulting in righteousness, and with the mouth he confesses, resulting in salvation."

'Confessing with our mouths that Jesus is Lord' is, I believe, the same as trusting in Him. Trusting in Him means we make Him Lord of our lives, and it is a visible thing; just as 'confessing with our mouths' is known to others. We live our lives as Jesus would have us live. To do that, though, means we have to shed our current way of living-our natural way of living, which conforms to our natural and of course, sinful desires. As the Bible puts it we must first repent of our sins. We must sincerely desire and strive with God's help to get rid of sin in our lives. **Repentance involves a conscious change in our lives, and it is absolutely essential to salvation**. Recall that John the Baptist went about baptizing the people in preparation for Jesus' ministry to begin, as the following passage indicates.

> Mark 1:4-5 "John the Baptist appeared in the wilderness **preaching a baptism of repentance for the forgiveness of sins**. And all the country of Judea was going out to him, and all the people of Jerusalem; and they were being baptized by him in the Jordan River, confessing their sins."

This preparation for Jesus involved repentance of sins, and so it does today. We cannot effectively 'trust Jesus' if we cling to our old ways. It is a lie to say that we are trusting Jesus if we continue to willfully do the things the Bible condemns. Now, here's the rub. We cannot break free of the sins in our lives unless we trust Jesus to help us. We are actually in bondage to sin in our lives until Jesus helps us to break free. We have to actually ask Jesus to help us break free of the sins in our lives, but not with crossed fingers behind our backs. We have to really mean it. First, however, we have to recognize the sins in our lives. I think that many people don't see the sins in their lives. The following 'tongue in cheek' statement by Jesus indicates this spiritual blindness.

> Luke 5:31-32 "And Jesus answered and said to them, "It is not those who are well who need a physician, but those who are sick. **I have not come to call the righteous but sinners to repentance."**

The irony of this statement is that nobody is righteous. "There is none righteous, not even one." (Rom 3:10) We are all sinners. So, what is Jesus saying? **He is saying that He can only heal those who know they are sinners.**

Now, with regard to sin, there are some sins that are difficult for us to avoid, while others do not present a problem. For example, some people have a real problem with lying, while other people find lying to be repulsive. Some people love to gossip, while others do not. Some people are trapped by lustful desires. Others are not. One thing is sure. Each one of us has at least one sin which is very difficult for us to avoid. The apostle Paul indicated this in his letter to the Hebrews.

> Hebrews 12:1-2 "…let us also lay aside every encumbrance, **and the sin which so easily entangles us,** and let us run with endurance the race that is set before us, fixing our eyes on Jesus, the author and perfecter of faith…"

The point of this discussion is this. You know and I know that even if we sincerely desire to rid our lives of the 'sin which so easily entangles,' we still do it on occasion. What's important, though, is that we struggle against it. We hate ourselves when we do it, and we don't give ourselves over to it. It (the sin) doesn't characterize us.

Notice that Paul told the Hebrews to fix their eyes on Jesus. We cannot sin if we truly do that. Remember the prayer I use when I am tempted? "Lord, please help me to hold my every thought captive for Jesus Christ." Without Jesus' help we are doomed to be in bondage to our sins.

When Jesus sent his disciples on a mission to proclaim the gospel message, repentance was part and parcel to that message. There can be no gospel or good news for the individual unless the person repents of his or her sins. Look at the following parallel passages-one from the book of Mark and one from the book of Luke.

> Mark 6:12-13 "And **they went out and preached that men should repent**. And they were casting out many demons and were anointing with oil many sick people and healing them."
>
> Luke 9:6 "And departing, **they began going about among the villages, preaching the gospel**, and healing everywhere."

Both accounts tell of the disciples preaching in villages. The Mark account focuses on the message of repentance. The Luke account focuses on the gospel message. I think one could accurately deduce that repentance is integral to the gospel message.

Sin is really a bad thing. It's so bad that Jesus had to be tortured and die on a Roman cross for our sins. It was the only remedy for sin. Otherwise no human being could be saved from eternal damnation. So, if Jesus died for our sins, do you see how ludicrous it would be for you or me to suppose that we could keep sin in our lives and still draw close to Jesus? No. We must, as the Bible says, die to our sin. The following passage says it quite well.

> Romans 6:6-7 "…knowing this, that our old self was crucified with Him, that our body of sin might be done away with, that we should no longer be slaves to sin; for he who has died is freed from sin."

Our old self must literally die, and we must be reborn with a spirit that longs to obey Christ. Look at the words Jesus spoke to a Pharisee named Nicodemus.

> John 3:3 "Jesus answered and said to him, "Truly, truly, I say to you, unless one is born again, he cannot see the kingdom of God."

We must become 'rewired' from the inside out. How do we do that, you might ask? It is something that must be granted to us from God. Otherwise it won't happen. God grants us repentance. He also leads us to Jesus, as the following passages indicate.

> Acts 11:18 "…God has granted to the Gentiles also the repentance that **leads to** life."
>
> John 6:44-45 "**No one can come to Me, unless the Father who sent Me draws him**; and I will raise him up on the **last** day. It is written in the prophets, 'And they shall be taught of God.' **Everyone who has heard and learned from the Father, comes to Me.**"(Jesus speaking)

We see in these passages that God leads us to repentance. More importantly, He leads us to Jesus. This is somewhat of a mystery to me, but I accept it. Some people will be led to Jesus, while others won't. If you are compelled to repent of your sins and follow Jesus, count yourself as being very fortu nate. No, it doesn't necessarily mean you are one of His elect, "For many are called, but few are chosen." (Matthew22:14). It means you have been called down the path that may lead you to salvation. What you do with that 'calling' is pretty much up to you. We will discuss this in more depth later.

We should now agree that repentance of our sins is essential to our salvation journey. It is essential to drawing close to and knowing Jesus Christ. Having repented we must next have and demonstrate faith in Jesus Christ. We have to do what He tells us to do. It is not sufficient to agree with Him and not alter our lives accordingly. However it is often difficult to apply Jesus' commands in our lives. Let's now discuss what it means to have and demonstrate faith in Jesus Christ.

Faith

I think we all have kind of an intuitive understanding of faith. To reiterate, it is to believe in something that is not yet seen. Let's revisit the Biblical definition of faith in the following passage:

> Hebrews 11:1 "Now faith is **the assurance of things hoped for**, the conviction of things not seen."

Faith is essential for our salvation. We have to trust and believe what God tells us to the extent we alter our lives, if necessary, to do what He tells us to do. The following passages give us some understanding of the importance God places on faith.

> Hebrews 10:38 "But my righteous one shall live by faith; and **if he shrinks back**, My soul has no pleasure in him."
>
> Hebrews 11:6 "And without faith it is impossible to please Him…"
>
> Romans 1:16-17 "For I am not ashamed of the gospel, for it is the power of God for salvation to everyone who believes, to the Jew first and also to the Greek. For in it **the righteousness of God is revealed from faith to faith;** as it is written, **"But the righteous man shall live by faith."**

This last passage supports the notion that we live a faith-filled journey toward salvation. So, specifically what should be the object of our faith; and how should our faith manifest itself? The Short answer to the first question is that Jesus Must be the object of our faith, as is indicated in the following passage:

> Galatians 2:20 "I have been crucified with Christ; and it is no longer I who live, but Christ lives in me; and **the life which I now live in the flesh I live by faith in the Son of God**, who loved me, and delivered Himself up for me."

Jesus must be the object of our faith, but the answer to 'how should our faith manifest itself' is critically influenced by how we characterize Jesus. If we properly characterize Him as the living Word of God, then our faith is manifest by reading and heeding the Bible. If our faith is real and sincere, it will reveal itself in our thoughts, words and deeds, which are called 'works' in the Bible. James, the half-brother of Jesus, author of the book of James and leader of the early Jerusalem church said the following about faith.

> James 2:14 "What use is it, my brethren, if a man says he has faith, but he has no works? Can that faith save him?"
>
> James 2:17 "Even so faith, if it has no works, is dead, being by itself."

Genuine faith will manifest itself in 'works.' The 'works' are evidence of faith. It is the faith that is evidenced by works that ultimately saves a person.

So, how do we acquire the faith that leads to salvation? The following passage gives us the answer.

> Romans 10:17 "So **faith comes from hearing**, and hearing by the word of Christ."

Real faith is the result of hearing the Word of God, the Bible. Read the Bible out loud. Listen to radio programs that teach the Bible. Listen to Bible CDs or tapes. I don't know why, but listening to Biblical passages is important to acquiring saving faith.

So, as we digest the Word of God by listening to and reading the Bible, God gives us the faith we need for our salvation journey. Just as God grants us repentance, He Also must grant us our faith. Otherwise we won't get it.

> Ephesians 2:8-10 "For by grace you have been saved through faith; and that not of yourselves, **it is the**

gift of God; not as a result of works, that no one should boast. For we are His workmanship, created in Christ Jesus for good works, which God prepared beforehand, that we should walk in them."

Now, here is a little bit of my personal observation on this matter of belief and faith. For years I went to church with my parents, and when I married and had children, we went to church as a family. I possessed a Bible all those years, but I never read it. Oh, I read a few passages here and there, but mostly it just sat on my shelf. Then, at some point in my life I believed that the Bible really was God's truth. I think I was helped to that conclusion through listening to radio programs such as Chuck Swindoll's 'Insight for Living' and J. Vernon McGee's 'Through the Bible Radio' program. Remember that 'faith comes from hearing and hearing by the Word of Christ.' After I sincerely believed the Bible to be God's truth, I started to read it in earnest. Then, God's wonderful truths literally leaped off the pages for me. It was as if my eyes were finally opened.

So, here's the point of this personal testimony. **The Bible must first be believed before it can be understood**. One cannot successfully approach the Bible with the notion of reading it to see if it has any merit. The person must believe it has merit prior to reading it. Then and only then will the person truly understand and benefit from what he or she is reading. So, my suggestion to you is to begin your journey of faith by listening to good Bible teachers such as Chuck Swindoll or J. Vernon McGee. It is somewhat of a 'leap of faith' to believe the Bible prior to reading it, but that's the essence of faith. As we demonstrate our faith to God, He will teach us and grant us even more faith. He will 'perfect' our faith. This is evidenced by the following passage.

> Hebrews 12:1-2 "...let us also lay aside every encumbrance, and the sin which so easily entangles us, and let us run with endurance the race that is set before us, fixing our eyes on Jesus, the author and **perfecter of faith**..."

As this passage implies, Jesus perfects our faith. Our faith is not stagnant. It should grow day by day. I believe the apostle Paul was referring to this in the following passage.

> Philippians 1:6 "For I am confident of this very thing, that **He who began a good work in you will perfect it until the day of Christ Jesus.**"

It is vitally important to remain close to Jesus, so that our faith will remain and grow even stronger. As we have already discussed, we need to 'abide in Jesus.' Apart from Jesus we cannot grow in our journey of faith, and we certainly cannot find salvation apart from Him. Paul again affirms this truth.

> Colossians 1:22-23 "...He has now reconciled you in His fleshly body through death, in order to present you before Him holy and blameless and beyond reproach-**if indeed you continue in the faith firmly established and steadfast, and not moved away from the <u>hope</u> of the gospel** that you have heard, which was proclaimed in all creation under heaven, and of which I, Paul, was made a minister."

Now then, you may be wondering, 'How does this saving faith actually manifest itself in my life? What does it look like on a day-to-day basis?' In the last section of this book I will provide some Biblical guidance on how we should live, but it's also beneficial at this point to provide some examples of 'right living.'

Living Right

Remember that the faith that saves is the faith that produces good works in a person's life. Good works are thoughts, words and deeds that are obedient to God's Word. This is true because faith in Jesus is faith in God's Word, the Bible. The Bible provides us with complete guidance on how to rightly live our lives. First of all it helps us to identify and avoid sin in our lives. **If we don't recognize sin, we certainly cannot avoid it.** Let's look at some passages that identify things to avoid in our lives.

> Romans 13:13-14 "Let us behave properly as in the day, not in carousing and drunkenness, not in sexual promiscuity and sensuality, not in strife and jealousy. But put on the Lord Jesus Christ, and make no provision for the flesh in regard to its lusts."
>
> Proverbs 20:19 "…do not associate with a gossip."
>
> Psalm 34:13-14 "Keep your tongue from evil, and your lips from speaking deceit. **Depart from evil and do good**; seek peace and pursue it."
>
> Isaiah 33:14-16 "Who among us can live with the consuming fire? Who among us can live with continual burning? **He who walks righteously, and speaks with sincerity, he who rejects unjust gain, and shakes his hands so that they hold no bribe; he who stops his ears from hearing about bloodshed, and shuts his eyes from looking upon evil.** He will dwell on the heights; his refuge will be the impregnable rock. His bread will be given him; his water will be sure."
>
> Ephesians 5:3-5 "But do not let immorality or any impurity or greed even be named among you,

as is proper among saints; and **there must be no filthiness and silly talk, or coarse jesting, which are not fitting, but rather giving of thanks.** For this you know with certainty, that **no immoral or impure person or covetous man, who is an idolator, has an inheritance in the kingdom of Christ and God."**

With these passages we have accumulated quite a list of 'don't do's' or things to avoid in our lives. These include carousing, drunkenness, sexual promiscuity, sensuality, strife, jealousy, gossiping, speaking evil, speaking deceit, looking upon evil, filthy talk, dirty jokes, and covetousness. There are many more 'don't do's' in the Bible, and I leave it to you to discover them for yourself. As I said before, some of these things are easy to avoid. Others are not. The beauty of the Bible is that is also provides us with ways or strategies to avoid these sins. It also gives us motivations to do the same. Let's look at some of these strategies and motivations.

> 2 Corinthians 10:5 "We are destroying speculations And every lofty thing raised up against the knowledge of God, and we are taking every thought captive to the obedience of Christ…"

As you may recall, I have already referred to this passage…twice. But I believe it is one of the most, if not the most effective strategies to avoid sin. The sin process begins in our minds. Look at what Jesus says.

> Mark 7:21-23 "For from within, out of the heart of men, proceed the evil thoughts, fornications, thefts, murders, adulteries, deeds of coveting and wickedness, as well as deceit, sensuality, envy, slander, pride and foolishness. All these evil things proceed from within and defile the man."

If we harbor and/or dwell on our evil thoughts, they will result in evil actions.

> James 1:14-15 "But each one is tempted when he is carried away and enticed by his own lust. Then when lust has conceived, it gives birth to sin; and when sin is accomplished it brings forth death."

Therefore, we must fight sin in our thought process. If we do that successfully, the sin will not manifest itself in words or actions. As a man, I consciously avert my eyes from looking on a woman who is not my wife. I do not ponder the material wealth of others, so as not to desire their possessions. I do not read newspaper articles about another person's evil deeds, knowing it might spark a desire of my own to sin. I change TV channels, so as not to look on or listen to things that may tempt me to sin. In other words, we can make conscious decisions to avoid things that might cause us to begin the sin process. We must control our thought process. We must direct our thoughts toward the right things. What things? Again, the Bible has the answer.

> Philippians 4:8 "Finally, brethren, whatever is true, whatever is honorable, whatever is right, whatever is pure, whatever is lovely, whatever is of good repute, if there is any excellence and if anything worthy of praise, let your mind dwell on these things."

There are many wonderful things on which we can focus our thoughts. We can think about God's creation, for example. We can think about a life well lived and a family that has benefited from it. We can think about another person's sacrifice that has benefited others. We can think about good experiences we have had in the past. These are but a few examples of how to direct our thoughts so as to avoid sin. However we must face another reality in our lives. We actually enjoy sinning because it brings pleasure to us.

As the Bible puts it, sin 'nourishes the flesh' but not in a healthy way. Our natural desire is to sin. It takes conscious effort not to sin. In fact, to be honest, we don't want to give it up. In the beginning of our Christian walk we may actually view God as some sort of 'cosmic killjoy' who wants us to give up all the fun things in our lives. So we honestly ask ourselves, "Is it possible to enjoy life without doing the sinful things we naturally want to do?" The short answer is, "Yes." Life can still be fun. In fact, it can be far richer and much more enjoyable without sin. Again, **it takes a leap of faith to give up the 'fun stuff' to gain real life**. In actuality it initially will seem like you are giving up your life, your wants and desires. However look at what Jesus says in this regard.

> Mark 8:34-36 "And He summoned the multitude with His disciples, and said to them, "If anyone wishes to come after Me, let him deny himself, and take up his cross, and follow Me. For whoever wishes to save his life shall lose it; but whoever loses his life for My sake and the gospel's shall save it. For what does it profit a man to gain the whole world, and forfeit his soul?"

Jesus says that in order to gain real life we must lose what we think is life. He isn't inferring that we actually kill ourselves. Rather, He is saying that we need to die to sinful pursuits. For example, let's say that I associate with a group of guys that indulge in sexual promiscuity, heavy drinking and dirty language. The Bible tells me not to do those things. So, if I turn away from those behaviors to be faithful to God's Word, I will have to stop associating with that group of friends. It will be a difficult thing to do if I really like those people. They won't understand and will probably take offense at my changed life. In all likelihood, I will be ostracized by that group. Initially, it will feel like I am losing my life for Jesus' sake. However that demonstration of true faith will lead to wonderful blessings in my life. As I lose my life of sin, God will transform me and grant me true life.

The Christian life is a life of growing in faith. It is a life characterized by change. We don't remain stagnant in our faith journey. Recall the following passage.

> Romans 12:1-2 "…present your bodies a living and holy sacrifice, acceptable to God, which is your spiritual service of worship. And **do not be conformed to this world, but be transformed by the renewing of your mind, that you may prove what the will of God is, that which is good and acceptable and perfect.**"

As we strive daily to be obedient to God's Word, God will transform us into the person He wants us to become. As we demonstrate our faith, God will grant us even more faith. And God will test our faith from time to time to see if it is genuine. This process will continue until we die, if we remain faithful.

> Philippians 1:6 "For I am confident of this very thing, that **He who began a good work in you will perfect it until the day of Christ Jesus.**"

So, we see that Christians are not perfect. They are not sin-free. They are people who are committed to a lifetime of spiritual change, a lifetime of spiritual alignment with Jesus Christ. One of my favorite bumper stickers is this one. 'Please be patient with me. God is not finished with me yet.' God will help us to align with Jesus. Again, this alignment is directed through the Word of God, the Bible. At this point we should raise a significant question. Do we have a part to play in the process, or does God do it all?

The current 'group think' in many churches is that people have no part to play in the salvation process. God does it all, so relax and enjoy the ride. However I think we do have a part to play. God provides the way to salvation, but I must accept it by faith. No, we are not saved by works. However works demonstrate our faith, as indicated in the following passage.

> Ephesians 2:8-10 "For **by grace you have been saved through faith**; and that not of yourselves, it is the gift of God; not as a result of works, that no one should boast. For **we are His workmanship, created in Christ Jesus for good works**, which God prepared beforehand, that we should walk in them."

Let's stop for a moment and look at the word, grace. What is grace? I once heard a very concise explanation of justice, mercy, and grace. Let me share it with you. From God's perspective, justice is getting what I deserve. Mercy is not getting what I deserve. Grace is getting what I don't deserve.

I am a sinner. I don't deserve salvation. I deserve judgment and an eternity in hell. However God will not send me to hell for the sins I have committed, **if** I believe and trust in Jesus Christ. Jesus paid for my sins on the cross.

His shed blood atoned for my sins, **if** I believe in Him. Notice the small word 'if.' I must believe in Jesus Christ in order for his shed blood to protect me from an eternity in hell. God's grace applies to giving me a way to avoid hell. My part in this process is to believe, and it must be genuine life changing belief. I do have a part to play, and at times it is not easy. Look at the following passages.

> 1 Peter 4:18 "And if **it is with difficulty that the righteous is saved**, what will become of the Godless man and the sinner?"
>
> Philippians 2:12-13 "…**work out your salvation with fear and trembling**; for it is God who is at work in you, both to will and to work for His good pleasure."

Throughout my life I will be faced with situations that will require me to make choices. Becoming aware of and believing in God's Truth doesn't remove my freedom of choice. However God's Truth will help me to make the right choices. In fact, my faith will be tested as long as I live on this earth. As with any test, I will either pass, or I will fail. In a nutshell, this freedom of choice we have is central to my premise that none of us can know if we will be saved. Why? Because we will always have the choice of turning away from God's truth. And who can know what their future decisions will be? Later, I will discuss this in depth. But for now, let's continue to concentrate on living rightly.

Love

We have looked at some of the 'don't do's' in the Bible, but there is another important side to living rightly. If we are truly faithful to the Bible, we will demonstrate love for God and the people God puts in our lives. Observe how Jesus summarized God's commandments.

> Mark 12:28-31 "…What commandment is the foremost of all?" Jesus answered, "The foremost is, 'Hear O Israel! The Lord our God is one Lord; and you shall love the Lord your God with all your heart, and with all your soul, and with all your mind, and with all your strength.' The second is this, 'You shall love your neighbor as yourself.' There is no other commandment greater than these."

Loving God

Let's look at the first commandment: '…love the Lord your God with all your heart, and with all your soul, and with all your mind, and with all your strength.' How do we do that? How does that love manifest itself in our lives? The answer is quite simple, really. The Bible says that **we demonstrate our love for God by doing what He tells us to do.** We don't demonstrate our love by waving our hands over our heads during a church service. We don't demonstrate our love by simply proclaiming we love God. No. We prove our love with the lives we lead. Properly demonstrating our love for God will require the total commitment of our hearts, souls, and minds; and yes, it will take all of our strength. Those that say that we have no part to play in our salvation have evidently not read this passage. Here are some Bible passages that tell us how to love God.

> 2 John 1:6 **"And this is love, that we walk according to His commandments."**

John 14:21 "**He who has My commandments and keeps them, he it is who loves Me**; and he who loves Me shall be loved by My Father, and I will love him, and will disclose Myself to him."

John 14:23 "Jesus answered and said to him, "**If anyone loves Me, he will keep My word**; and My Father will love him, and We will come to him, and make Our abode with him."

So, we see that there is only one way to love God, and that is to obey His commandments. How do we know what He commands us to do? There is only one way to know His commandments. That is to read the Bible. I believe that loving God with all of our minds means to diligently and daily study the Bible. The Bible needs to be the guiding light for our lives. There is no other guiding light. It is our only reliable source of truth; and **all of our decisions are rightly made only in light of what the Bible says**.

At this point you may be thinking, 'there are many commandments in the old testament that would be difficult to obey,' or 'how do I know which commandments apply today?' I acknowledge that discernment is needed to answer those legitimate concerns. For example, during the exodus from Egypt, God commanded the Israelites to kill an unruly child who wouldn't obey his or her parents. While we may at times think this is a good idea, it wouldn't be allowed in today's society. Yet, undeniably it was one of God's commands. Again, we must have discernment to know how to rightly obey God's commands. Basically, we need help. And this help comes to us in the form of the Holy Spirit, as this next Bible passage indicates.

> John 14:15-17 "If you love Me, you will keep My commandments. And I will ask the Father, and He will give you another Helper, that He may be with you forever; that is the Spirit of truth, whom the world cannot receive, because it does not behold Him or know Him, but you know Him because He abides with you, and will be in you."

When we become 'believers,' the Bible says that God's Holy Spirit comes to us, to be with us, to guide us, and to teach us. Now, I don't have an inside track on how the Holy Spirit works or how He will guide us. But I do know that He does. He has guided me on many occasions. He has reminded me of Scripture passages that have helped me in difficult times. He has referred me to other Scripture passages that have illuminated a difficult to understand passage. With regard to the previous example of the unruly and disobedient child, I have deduced from Scripture that there was no forgiveness for willful sin in early Israel. There was no allowance even for repentance. The offending party could cry his eyes out and beg for mercy, but to no avail. Jesus Christ's atoning death on the cross later provided the only way for people to repent of their sins and be forgiven.

Loving Our Neighbor

Now that we have some idea of how we demonstrate our love for God, we next turn to demonstrating love for 'our neighbor' or the people who come into our lives. We are to 'love our neighbor as ourselves.' What does that mean? The obvious answer is that we nurture and care for others just as we do for ourselves. I don't think it means that we comb other people's hair, although it might in some cases mean just that. Rather, I believe it mandates an attitude that we have toward others, an attitude that produces right thoughts, words and actions toward others. I think the best description of love toward others was expressed by the apostle Paul in the following passage.

> 1 Corinthians 13:4-8 "Love is patient, love is kind, and is not jealous; love does not brag and is not arrogant, does not act unbecomingly; it does not seek its own, is not provoked, does not take into account a wrong suffered, does not rejoice in unrighteousness, but rejoices with the truth; bears all things, believes all things, hopes all things, endures all things. Love never fails…"

In fact, Paul's description of love applies most appropriately to the most important human relationship we can have-marriage. I believe marriage is a microcosm of our relationship with God. From personal experience, I have come to realize that my love for my wife is a conscious choice demonstrated through my words and actions. Sometimes it is difficult to demonstrate that love; sometimes it is not. It is the same in my relationship with God. Sometimes it is difficult to obey Him; sometimes it is not. However God commands me to love my wife, just as He commands me to love Him. It is not an option to love only if I feel like it. Rather, it is a command and a demonstration of my obedience and fidelity. I have also discovered that right feelings follow right actions. When I am obedient to God by loving my wife even when I don't feel like it, He rewards me with the feelings of love as well.

How then do we demonstrate love for the people around us? The Bible has much to say about how we are to love others. First of all, the Bible speaks about the attitude we should have toward others in the following passage.

> Philippians 2:3-4 "Do nothing from selfishness or empty conceit, but with humility of mind **let each of you regard one another as more important than himself; do not merely look out for your own personal interests, but also for the interests of others.**"

Now, I'm going to be right up front with you and admit that I don't obey this command very well on a daily basis. I know that I am basically a very selfish person…remember those sins that so easily entangle? Well, this is one of mine. I pray frequently for the Lord to help me in this area, and it's slow going. However from time to time I surprise myself and actually prioritize another person's needs. My wife does this very well, and I admire her for it. She is a good example for me, and it (my weakness) is probably one of the reasons God brought her into my life. Now, does the fact that I am selfish mean that I will not reach salvation? Maybe it does, but not necessarily. I believe we are required to struggle against our sins. We are never to be content with ourselves. This journey toward salvation is a continual struggle, and as long as we consistently struggle, I think we are on the right path. Let's look at another passage.

> 1 John 3:17-18 "But whoever has the world's goods, and beholds his brother in need and closes his heart against him, how does the love of God abide in him? Little children, **let us not love with word or with tongue, but in deed and truth.**"

I don't believe that we are called to help all the needy people in the world. However I think that God makes us aware of those we should help. Another way to say it is that God 'convicts' us of things we should do on behalf of others. It might be the beggar on the street. It might literally be our neighbor who lost a job and needs a financial boost. It might be a relative in need. It might be a disaster somewhere in the world. Whatever the situation, I have found that God moves me to help certain ones. I think we need to become sensitive to God's leading and convicting. But how do we recognize God's leading?

I have discovered that God doesn't speak in a loud distinct voice. He speaks in a very gentle whisper-a whisper that I can ignore or obey. I have also discovered that if I ignore the whisper, I grow increasingly uncomfortable. The discomfort ceases when I follow His guidance. Unfortunately, it also ceases when I let the world and all of its confusion distract me and take me away from that wonderful moment of communication with my Lord. I can look back at those brief moments when I didn't follow the Lord's leading, and in so doing I can revisit the discomfort and disappointment I felt when I didn't listen to Him. Opportunities to help others sometimes appear only for a moment, requiring an immediate decision on our part. We must be prepared to decide correctly. There is a wonderful Biblical example of how God speaks when He revealed Himself to Elijah. Let's look at that passage.

> 1 Kings 19:11-13 "So He said, "Go forth and stand on the mountain before the Lord." And behold, the Lord was passing by! And a great and strong wind was rending the mountains and breaking in pieces the rocks before the Lord; but the Lord was not in

the wind. And after the wind an earthquake, but the Lord was not in the earthquake. And after the earthquake a fire, but the Lord was not in the fire; and after the fire a sound of a gentle blowing. And it came about when Elijah heard it, that he wrapped his face in his mantle, and went out and stood in the entrance of the cave. And behold, a voice came to him and said, "What are you doing here, Elijah?"

We see from this example that God appeared to Elijah in a very subtle way, and Elijah recognized it was God. Elijah was 'in tune' with God because he spoke for God on earth. Elijah was a Prophet, a person chosen by God to relay God's messages to the people. Today God doesn't use Prophets. He uses the Bible. However, we must be 'in tune' with Him to hear and /or understand His messages. Let's look at another passage that tells us how to love others.

> Romans 12:9-21 "Let love be without hypocrisy. Abhor what is evil; cling to what is good. Be devoted to one another in brotherly love; give preference to one another in honor; not lagging behind in diligence, fervent in spirit, serving the Lord; rejoicing in hope, persevering in tribulation, devoted to prayer; contributing to the needs of the saints, practicing hospitality. Bless those who persecute you; bless and curse not. Rejoice with those who rejoice, and weep with those who weep. Be of the same mind toward one another; do not be haughty in mind, but associate with the lowly. Do not be wise in your own estimation. Never pay back evil for evil to anyone. Respect what is right in sight of all men. If possible, so far as it depends on you, be at peace with all men. Never take your own revenge, beloved, but leave room for the wrath of God, for

> it is written, "Vengeance is Mine, I will repay," says the Lord. "But if your enemy is hungry, feed him, and if he is thirsty, give him a drink; for in so doing you will heap burning coals upon his head." Do not be overcome by evil, but overcome evil with good."

This passage is rich in guidance on how to treat others. It really speaks for itself. Humility and generosity appear to be two important characteristics in loving others. It also appears that we need to keep our anger under control. We are also called to not 'get even' with those who have wronged us. We are rather to treat them well. We must leave the 'getting even' with God. Understandably, these may not be 'natural' responses for us, but they do produce the best results.

The Bible has much more to say with regard to loving others, and I leave it to you to find those passages. However I don't think we should leave this section without knowing the importance that God places on loving others. Look at the following passage.

> 1 John 4:20-21 "If someone says, "I love God," and hates his brother, he is a liar; for the one who does not love his brother whom he has seen, cannot love God whom he as not seen. And this commandment we have from Him, that the one who loves God should love his brother also."

Thus far we have seen that the pathway to salvation involves believing in and trusting Jesus. Elements that are essential to that belief and trust are repentance, faith, reading and heeding the Bible, living right and loving God and others. This is a difficult pathway for any person to walk, and it is even more difficult if we do it on our own.

We need others to encourage us to stay the course and to help us up when we are down. To this end, Jesus gave us His church, the collective or body of believers in Jesus Christ.

The Church

Like many other words in Christianity, I believe that the word, church, has been misused and misunderstood. I'll wager that the majority of people think of a building when they hear the word, church. They may combine the notion of a building with the activities conducted therein, but by and large, church is characterized as a building. The Bible describes church differently. Look at the following passages.

> 1 Corinthians 16:19 "The churches of Asia greet you. Aquila and Prisca greet you heartily in the Lord, with the church that is in their house."
>
> Ephesians 1:22-23 "And He (God) put all things in subjection under His (Jesus') feet, and gave Him (Jesus) as head over all things to the church, which is His body, the fullness of Him who fills all in all."

The first passage described a group of people who met in a particular house as being a church. So, we see that the church really is a group of people-not a building. More specifically, it is a group of people who share their belief in Jesus Christ.

The second passage demonstrates that Jesus Christ is the head of the church. He is the head of the collective body of believers. And this body of believers is also characterized as the body of Jesus. Remember that true believers abide in Jesus. This is another way to describe 'abiding in Jesus.' And like a body with many parts, each of us has a part to play in that body for the benefit of the entire body. Each of us serves to keep the body healthy and intact. In these next passages, Paul suggests some ways that we help the body of believers.

> Hebrews 10:24-25 "…and let us consider how to stimulate one another to love and good deeds, not forsaking our own assembling together, as is the habit of some, but encouraging one another; and all the more, as you see the day drawing near."
>
> Colossians 3:16 "Let the word of Christ richly dwell within you, with all wisdom teaching and admonishing one another with psalms and hymns and spiritual songs, singing with thankfulness in your hearts to God."
>
> 1 Corinthians 14:26 "What is the outcome then, brethren? When you assemble, each one has a psalm, has a teaching, has a revelation, has a tongue, has an interpretation. Let all things be done for edification."

The last passage tells us to 'edify' each other. This means that we improve each other morally, and we benefit each other spiritually by educating and encouraging one another. As I said, this salvation journey is not easy. We may have a burst of spiritual energy for a while, but it is difficult to sustain for the duration. So, we need other like-minded believers to encourage us and to renew our spiritual energy.

In a nutshell, I think the primary purpose of the church is to help believers persevere in their salvation journey. However, over the years the church has taken on other roles. Some have benefited the collective of believers, and some have not. I think the proper church model was exhibited in the very early church. The following passage gives us a picture of early church activity.

> Acts 2:42 "And they were continually devoting themselves to the apostles' teaching and to fellowship, to the breaking of bread and to prayer."

The early believers had fellowship with each other, continued to learn about Jesus and prayed a lot. This was a very simple but effective venue. They were steeped in the Word of God, which strengthened and encouraged them. Later, more and more rules were introduced, and churches became more restrictive. They began to depart from their first love, becoming more restrictive in their worship, and eventually the people were put in bondage to religion. This has been very harmful and has severely weakened the church. Jesus issued a subtle warning to the apostle Peter about the potential of this bondage in the following passage.

> Matthew 16:18-19 "And I also say to you that you are Peter, and upon this rock I will build My church; and the gates of Hades shall not overpower it. I will give you the keys of the kingdom of heaven; and whatever you shall bind on earth shall be bound in heaven, and whatever you shall loose on earth shall be loosed in heaven."

Many believe that Jesus gave Peter the keys to the 'pearly gates' in this passage. I disagree. I think Jesus was saying that Peter could organize the church in such a way that he could put people in bondage or he could keep them free in their faith. Jesus did not encourage bondage, as the following passage indicates.

> Galatians 5:1 "It was for freedom that Christ set us free; therefore keep standing firm and do not be subject again to a yoke of slavery."

In addition to becoming enslaved to sin in our lives, we can also become enslaved to religion. Why? I think we become enslaved because religion uses superstition to control the masses; and superstition is a part of our sinful makeup. Satan knows this, and he has done some of his most effective work using superstition in religion.

I don't mean to pick on Roman Catholics, but have you ever noticed what the people do when the priest sprinkles 'holy water' on them? They instantly make the sign of the cross. That, in my opinion, is a graphic example of superstition at work. First of all, they think the water has some magical properties. Secondly, they think making the sign of the cross will somehow bring God's favor. Neither of these beliefs is Biblical. They have been created in the religion.

For this and other reasons I reject religion. I am very offended if someone characterizes me as religious. I would rather be characterized as a disciple of Jesus Christ-a follower of The Way.

So then, how do we benefit from the church today? Where do we find a church that serves the purpose of encouraging and edifying believers? First of all, I believe we should pray for God to lead us to other believers. How many other believers do we need? Jesus said, "…where two or three have gathered together in My name, there I am in their midst." (Matthew 18:20) We don't need a large collection of people to have a church. However I do think the church needs to be Biblically based.

If you find a church that adds to or takes away from what the Bible says, don't stay. Look for another one. What should a good church do? It should teach, it should read Scripture, it should encourage and nurture believers and it should pray; much like the early church.

Before we leave this section devoted to articulating the pathway to salvation as it is taught in the Bible, we should briefly summarize the points we have discussed. The Bible tells us we must believe in Jesus Christ to be saved. However in order to rightly believe in Him, we must rightly characterize Him. The only way to rightly characterize Jesus is to read the Bible. However we must first believe the Bible to be true before we read it. Otherwise we won't understand it. We must sincerely desire not to sin anymore.

We must give up the momentary pleasures of sin. With the help of the Holy Spirit, we must actually live our lives according to how the Bible tells us to live. We must demonstrate our Love for God by doing what He tells us to do. We must also demonstrate Biblical love for others. Finally, we must find other like-minded believers to help us to stay on the pathway toward salvation.

There appears to be a long and cumbersome list of things to do to gain our salvation, but all of these things are part and parcel to believing in Jesus. If you look carefully at this list you will see that a most crucial step in the process is to believe the Bible is true. If you do that, the rest falls in line. All of these things simply define what it means to believe in Jesus.

The Paths Away From Salvation

As we have seen, there is only one way to salvation... through Jesus Christ. Unfortunately, there are many paths away from salvation. There are many pathways that will lead to hell. Jesus summed it up well in the following passage.

> Matthew 7:13-14 "Enter by the narrow gate; for **the gate is wide, and the way is broad that leads to destruction, and many are those who enter by it. For the gate is small, and the way is narrow that leads to life, and few are those who find it.**"

This is a very sobering passage, which contains two very important truths. First, it tells us that most people are going to hell. Secondly, it tells us that it is difficult to even find the way to heaven. So, then what are we to do? Do we give up because it is too difficult? No. We must indeed seek the narrow way to the small gate, and we must avoid the broad way that leads to destruction. How do we do that? Again, the Bible is our only source of truth in this matter. It defines the ways to destruction, so that we can avoid them. I sincerely believe that God will lead us on the narrow 'pathway of righteousness' that leads to the small gate, if we truly try to avoid the pathways to destruction. When we sincerely and diligently strive to follow the path of righteousness, the Bible tells us that God will lead us to the gate that leads to salvation. Look at the following passage.

> 2 Peter 1:10-11 "…be all the more certain about His calling and choosing you; for as long as you practice these things, you will never stumble; for in this way the entrance into the eternal kingdom of our Lord and Savior Jesus Christ will be abundantly supplied to you."

The Ways to Destruction

Let's look again at some of the things we are to avoid.

> Galatians 5:19-21 "Now the deeds of the flesh are evident, which are: **immorality, impurity, sensuality, idolatry, sorcery, enmities, strife, jealousy, outbursts of anger, disputes, dissensions, factions, envying, drunkenness, carousing, and things like these,** of which I forewarn you just as I have forewarned you that **those who practice such things shall not inherit the kingdom of God.**"

This passage has, as we have said before, a long list of 'don't do's.' However, I want to call your attention to the word 'practice' in the last sentence. I believe the sins that will lead a person to hell are the one's that characterize that person. They are the sins that are part of that person's daily life. They are the sins for which the person does not repent. Now, here's the difficulty. Many do not recognize sin as sin. In fact some people think that the sins they are committing are blessed by God, as is evidenced by the following passage.

> Isaiah 5:20 "Woe to those who call evil good, and good evil..."

Let's look at an example. Some people think that a 'loving' and committed homosexual relationship is blessed by God. With this notion they are actually calling evil good. They have not read and/or believed the following Bible passage.

> 1 Corinthians 6:9-10 "Or do you not know that the unrighteous shall not inherit the kingdom of God? Do not be deceived; neither fornicators, nor idolators, nor adulterers, nor effeminate, nor homosexuals, nor thieves, nor the covetous, nor drunkards, nor revilers, nor swindlers, shall inherit the kingdom of God."

Now, I don't want to take away hope from the person who believes he or she is a homosexual. The sin is not in the 'being.' It is in the 'doing.' I believe a homosexual person can live a life that honors God, if they don't engage in homosexual activity. A homosexual marriage or relationship is contrary to what the Bible commands. Recall the proof of our love for God is to do what He commands of us, and His commands are found in the Bible.

Not to keep picking on the homosexual community, but they provide another excellent example of a human tendency. When we don't find an answer we like, sometimes we look elsewhere for a more palatable answer. Some in this community have formed or found churches that affirm their homosexual relationships. They overlook or disavow the truth of Biblical Scripture and tell each other they are on solid footing. Look at the following passage. God knows us so well.

> 2 Timothy 4:3-4 "For the time will come when they will not endure sound doctrine; but wanting to have their ears tickled, **they will accumulate for themselves teachers in accordance to their own desires; and will turn away their ears from the truth and will turn aside to myths.**"

Denying God's truth will not make it go away. We can live a lie and think everything is OK. However when we die we will face an eternity of agony and pain. I like the gravity analogy. A man once decided he wouldn't believe in gravity and jumped off the roof of a very tall building. Halfway down in his 'free fall' another man stuck his head out of a window and asked the falling man how it was going. The falling man said, 'so far, so good.' That's the way many perceive their lives of sin... 'so far, so good.' Perhaps we should see what the Bible says about the 'sudden stop' at the end.

> Revelation 21:7-8 "**He who overcomes shall inherit these things, and I will be his God and he will be My son. But for the cowardly and unbelieving and abominable and murderers and immoral persons and sorcerers and idolaters and all liars, their part will be in the lake that burns with** fire and brimstone, which is the second **death."**
>
> 2 Thessalonians 1:7-9 "...the Lord Jesus shall be revealed from heaven with His mighty angels in flaming fire, dealing out retribution **to those who do not know God and to those who do not obey the gospel of our Lord Jesus**. And these He will pay the penalty of eternal destruction, away from the presence of the Lord and from the glory of His power..."

The Bible is pretty clear. There is a hell and there is a heaven, and we will reside in one of those places for all eternity. The span of our lives here on Earth is a mere breath compared to eternity. I once heard a very good explanation of eternity.

Imagine a bird that is able to fly from here to the moon and back. Imagine that bird taking one grain of sand from all the sand on the earth and flying it to the moon and dropping it off. Imaging the bird then flying back to the earth to get another single grain of sand and repeating the process, until all the sand on the earth has been moved to the moon. Then, imagine the bird moving all the sand back to the earth in the same manner. The time required for the bird to accomplish that incredibly long task is but a brief moment in eternity. Wouldn't it be better to spend eternity in heaven rather than hell? Wouldn't it be worth giving up the pleasures of sin for a brief lifetime to avoid an eternal sentence in agony?

Let's look at a few more passages that tell us things that will lead us to destruction, so that we may avoid them. There are many more Biblical passages than the one's I will list, and I leave it to you to find them as you study your Bible.

> Matthew 15:18-20 "But the things that proceed out of the mouth come from the heart, and those defile the man. For out of the heart come evil thoughts, murders, adulteries, fornications, thefts, false witness, slanders. These are the things which defile the man…"

> Proverbs 6:16-19 "There are six things which the Lord hates, yes, seven which are an abomination to Him: haughty eyes, a lying tongue, and hands that shed innocent blood, a heart that devises wicked plans, feet that run rapidly to evil, a false witness who utters lies, and one who spreads strife among brothers."

These passages contain quite a list of things that will lead one to destruction. Indeed **there are many pathways to hell, but only one pathway to heaven**. As I mentioned previously, it is not easy to remain on the pathway to heaven.

It takes a daily commitment to faith in Jesus Christ and help from the Holy Spirit to persevere successfully. We will encounter many tests of our faith along the way; and as with any test it is possible to pass. It is also possible to fail. At all points in our lives we have the choice to either persevere or to turn away from following Jesus. Quite frankly, we can't possible know which way we will choose in the future. The Bible has numerous examples of those who have turned away from their faith, and we should look at some of these.

Falling From Grace

Let me again bring to mind the thesis of this book. There are some people who have been chosen by God to gain salvation when they die. These people are called the elect. Mankind does not know who these people are. Only God knows. As we proceed on our journey of faith in this life, others may tell us that our salvation is assured. We may even think we know we are of God's elect. However we don't know what the future will hold. We don't know the trials that are ahead of us. We don't know how we will respond to those trials. We can choose to be faithful to God's Word in those trials. We can also choose to depart from the faith. In the following passages the Bible talks about some who have chosen to depart from the faith.

> 1 Timothy 4:1 "But the Spirit explicitly says that in later times **some will fall away from the faith**, paying attention to deceitful spirits and doctrines of demons…"
>
> 2 Peter 3:17-18 "…be on your guard lest, being carried away by the error of unprincipled men, **you fall from your own steadfastness,** but grow in the

grace and knowledge of our Lord and Savior Jesus Christ."

Hebrews 3:12 "Take care brethren, lest there should be in a one of you an evil, unbelieving heart, in **falling away** from the living God."

These passages clearly indicate that some were 'in the faith;' but for whatever reason, they decided to depart from the faith. The 'assurance teachers' will tell you that these people were not true believers to begin with. True. However while they were 'in the faith,' they appeared to everyone, including themselves, to be true believers. While they were 'in the faith' they did not foresee the event(s) that would make them choose to fall away. Neither can we.

Many churches today have what is called an 'alter call.' If you have ever watched a Billy Graham TV special, you will see that he finishes with an alter-call. The alter-call signifies the moment that an individual makes a decision for Jesus Christ. I think it is a good thing, but I don't think it needs to be done in public to be valid. The decision can be made anywhere, at any time. The point I want to make here is that the preacher making the 'alter call' generally asks the people, 'Do you want to know that you will spend an eternity in heaven? If you make a decision for Jesus Christ, at this moment you can know you have that eternity.'

The alter-call message leads the person to believe that they have gained salvation, and nothing can remove it. This is a flawed message that leads to confusion in that person's life, because they still have the freedom of choice to depart from their newly found faith. Jesus' parable about the 'different soils' spoke about the various types of people who have entered the faith. Let's look at a section from that parable.

> Mark 4:16-17 "And in a similar way these are the ones on whom seed was sown on the rocky places, who, **when they hear the word, immediately receive it with joy**; and they have no firm root in themselves, but are only temporary; then, when affliction or persecution arises because of the word, immediately they fall away."

These people made an 'alter-call,' but their faith didn't last. They didn't know that they would have to endure hardships that would test and strengthen their faith. They evidently weren't of God's elect, but the preacher didn't know it. Neither did they.

I have heard some of the 'assurance teachers' characterize 'believers' that lapse into a sinful life as 'carnal Christians.' These 'Christians,' they say, are not in danger of losing out on salvation. However they may not receive as many rewards in heaven as other well-behaved Christians. Hogwash. A more suitable name for a 'carnal Christian' is 'unbeliever.' God is pretty clear on the results of our choices after making a decision to have faith in Jesus Christ. Look at the following passages.

> Ezekiel 18:24 "But when a righteous man turns away from his righteousness, commits iniquity, and does according to all the abominations that a wicked man does, will he live? **All his righteous deeds which he has done will not be remembered for his treachery which he has committed and his sin which he has committed; for them he will die.**"

> Ezekiel 33:18-19 "**When the righteous turns from his righteousness and commits iniquity, then he shall die in it.** But when the wicked turns from his wickedness and practices justice and righteousness, he will live by them."

I think it is pretty serious business to become a 'believer,' enjoying the spiritual benefits of being a 'believer;' and then to choose to depart from the faith. In fact, the Bible says that it is difficult if not impossible to return to the faith. Look at the following sobering passages.

> Hebrews 6:4-6 "For in the case of **those who have once been enlightened** and have tasted of the heavenly gift and have been made partakers of the Holy Spirit, and have tasted the good word of God and the powers of the age to come, and **then have fallen away, it is impossible to renew them again to repentance**, since they again crucify to themselves the Son of God, and put Him to open shame."

> 2 Peter 2:20-21 "For **if after they have escaped** the defilements of the world by the knowledge of the Lord and Savior Jesus Christ, **they are again entangled in them** and are overcome, **the last state has become worse for them than the first**. For it would be better for them not to have known the way of righteousness, than having known it, to turn away from the holy commandment delivered to them."

Now, I know that some will point out to me the parable of the prodigal son. It is found in Luke 15:11-32 if you want to read it. The story is about a man's youngest son who left home to live in sin. Later, he returned with a repentant heart and was forgiven by his father. This is not analogous to someone departing from the faith and then returning. First of all, the young son hadn't rejected sin with a repentant heart prior to leaving his home. It wasn't like he was returning to sin that he had previously rejected. No. He had always longed for the sin. Only when he experienced the reality of a sinful lifestyle did he choose to repent. I guess you could say in an analogous fashion that the young son was one of the elect. However like all of the elect, he began his faith journey at some point in his life when he chose to repent of all sin in his life.

Having discussed 'falling from grace,' we will next turn to an equally important discussion about those who appear to be 'saved.' I am speaking of those who by their position or appearance appear to be headed for heaven. People around them are convinced of their secure position. More significantly, they themselves are convinced.

Those Who Appear To Be Saved

You know the people about whom I am speaking. They are the ministers, the preachers, the pastors, the priests, the people who attend church regularly, the people who wear Christian symbols and put them on their cars. They are also the TV evangelists. Now, I am not saying that these people will not go to heaven. I am saying that none of them can know for certain that they will.

In speaking about those individuals who appear to be saved, I would be remiss if I didn't include the example of the Pharisees. The Pharisees were the religious leaders of Jesus' time, and I don't think anybody would have dared to question their salvation. They 'worked for and represented God.' However, Jesus demonstrated nothing but contempt for this group of individuals. Look at how Jesus viewed and spoke to them.

> Matthew 23:27-28 "Woe to you scribes and Pharisees, hypocrites! For you are like whitewashed tombs which on the outside appear beautiful, but

inside they are full of dead men's bones and all uncleanness. Even so you too outwardly appear righteous to men, but inwardly you are full of hypocrisy and lawlessness."

Mark 7:6-9 "And He said to them, "Rightly did Isaiah prophesy of you hypocrites, as it is written, 'This people honors Me with their lips, but their heart is far away from Me. But in vain do they worship Me, teaching as doctrines the precepts of men.' Neglecting the commandments of God, you hold to the traditions of men." He was also saying to them, "You nicely set aside the commandment of God in order to keep your tradition."

Matthew 5:20 "For I say to you, that unless your righteousness surpasses that of the scribes and Pharisees, you shall not enter the kingdom of heaven."

Jesus was not fooled by the outward religious appearance of the Pharisees. He saw right through them to their rotten core. They were a proud group. They were blind to the sins in their lives and were unrepentant. They believed they represented God here on Earth. They even thought they were representing God when they had Jesus killed. What an irony. Are there Pharisees in religion today? I think so.

Religious leaders don't have an inside track to salvation. Like you and me, these people must persevere in their faith to the end of their lives to be saved. Their outward appearance will not save them. Let's revisit a Biblical passage that speaks to this.

Matthew 7:21-23 "**Not everyone who says to Me, 'Lord, Lord,' will enter the kingdom of heaven; but he who does the will of My Father who is in**

heaven. Many will say to Me on that day, 'Lord, Lord, did we not prophesy in Your name, and in your name cast out demons, and in Your name perform many miracles?' And then I will declare to them, **"I never knew you; depart from Me, you who practice lawlessness."**

About whom was Jesus speaking? I believe He was speaking about religious leaders. These people actually used Jesus' name to do many magnificent things. They probably even drew many people to Jesus. The problem was that they never really knew Jesus themselves. They probably had sin in their lives for which they had never repented.

This brings up a very important question. Is it possible to lead others toward salvation and fail to make it there ourselves? I say that is definitely possible. The apostle Paul realized this, as is indicated in the following passage.

> 1 Corinthians 9:27 "…I buffet my body and make it my slave, lest possibly, after I have preached to others, I myself should be **disqualified**."

Paul realized that salvation was a reward granted only at the end of a life whose latter part was characterized by true faith in Jesus Christ. He also realized that one cannot 'rest on one's laurels.' A person's rank within a religious organization is not sufficient for salvation. However members of a religious organization may tell one another that their salvation is assured. Paul also spoke to this mindset in the following passage.

> 2 Corinthians 10:12 "For we are not bold to class or compare ourselves with some of those who commend themselves; but when they measure

themselves by themselves, and compare themselves with themselves, they are without understanding."

The Bible demonstrates that God is disgusted with much of religion. He sees the rituals and external displays that some people think will please God. But as the following passages indicate, God knows the hearts that are directed toward Him. He also knows the hearts that are turned away. Look at what He says.

> Matthew 15:8-9 "This people honors Me with their lips, but their heart is far away from Me. But **in vain do they worship Me**, teaching as doctrines the precepts of men."
>
> Amos 5:21-24 "I hate, I reject your festivals, nor do I delight in your solemn assemblies. Even though you offer up to Me burnt offerings and your grain offerings, I will not accept them; and I will not even look at the peace offerings of your fatlings. Take away from Me the noise of your songs; I will not even listen to the sound of your harps. But **let justice roll down like waters and righteousness like an ever-flowing stream**."
>
> Isaiah 1:13-17 "Bring your worthless offerings no longer. Incense is an abomination to Me. New moon and Sabbath, the calling of assemblies-I cannot endure iniquity and the solemn assembly. I hate your new moon festivals and your appointed feasts. They have become a burden to Me. I am weary of bearing them. So when you spread out your hands in prayer, I will hide My eyes from you. Yes, **even though you multiply prayers, I will not listen**. Your hands are covered with blood. **Wash yourselves, make yourselves clean**; remove the evil of your

deeds from My sight. Cease to do evil. Learn to do good. Seek justice, reprove the ruthless; defend the orphan, plead for the widow."

One can conclude from these passages that God doesn't want religion. He wants people who have repentant and obedient hearts toward Him. And He doesn't want obedience only for a season. He wants. No. He demands it forever. Look at this next passage.

> Ezekiel 33:12 "The righteousness of a righteous man will not deliver him in the day of his transgression…"

For this reason no one can know for certain that they will reach salvation. No one can know if they will be successfully obedient to God in the future. They can only hope they will. In the next section I will discuss in more depth the notion that no person can know for certain that they will be saved.

We Cannot Know For Certain We Will Be Saved

The apostle Paul really set an example for all of us regarding the attitude we should have in our salvation journey. Paul realized that even though he was committed to doing the Lord's work, his salvation was not assured. He knew that he could not let down his guard and let his natural sinful nature take control. He knew that his attitude had to be one of hope rather than assurance. Look at what Paul said.

> Romans 8:23-25 "And not only this, but also we ourselves, having the first fruits of the Spirit, even we ourselves groan within ourselves, waiting eagerly for our adoption as sons, the redemption of our

> body. **For in hope we have been saved, but hope that is seen is not hope; for why does one also hope for what he sees? But if we hope for what we do not see, with perseverance we wait eagerly for it.**"
>
> Philippians 3:11-14 "…in order that I may attain to the resurrection from the dead. **Not that I have already obtained it, or have already become perfect, but I press on in order that I may lay hold of that for which also I was laid hold of by Christ Jesus. Brethren, I do not regard myself as having laid hold of it yet; but one thing I do: forgetting what lies behind and reaching forward to what lies ahead, I press on toward the goal for the prize of the upward call of God in Christ Jesus.**"

Let's stop for a moment and reflect on Hope. Hope is a good thing. It is not and should not be discouraging or troubling for anybody to know that they have a hope for salvation. While hope is not assurance, I believe that it is almost assurance. Scripture tells us that we can know our relationship with the Lord at any moment. As the apostle John tells us, "We know that we have passed out of death into life, because we love the brethren."(1 John 3:14). And Jesus said, "Truly, truly, I say to you, **he who believes has eternal life**."(John 6:47)

We can know our present relationship with the Lord. What we cannot know is our future relationship with the Lord. Why? Because we still have freedom of choice. It is still possible, however unlikely, for any of us to choose to depart from our faith, as the following passage indicates.

> 1Timothy 4:1 "But the Spirit explicitly says that in later times some will fall away from the faith, paying attention to deceitful spirits and doctrines of demons."

Some of you may be thinking, "If I have eternal life, doesn't that mean I have salvation?" Recall the Biblical definition of eternal life. Jesus defined it for us in John 17:3 when He said, "And this is eternal life, that they may know Thee, the only true God, and Jesus Christ whom Thou hast sent." To know Jesus, one has to abide in Jesus through an active faith and focus on the Word of God. If we departed from that active faith and diligent focus on the Word of God, I believe we would depart from knowing Jesus. If we depart from knowing Jesus, the logical conclusion is that we would no longer have 'eternal life.' I know that the word 'eternal' creates confusion. However I think it is most important to focus on Jesus' definition rather than Webster's dictionary.

Let's look at other Bible passages that tell us we have a hope for salvation that will survive only if we persevere in our faith.

> Hebrews 3:12-14 "Take care, brethren, lest there should be in a one of you an evil, unbelieving heart, in **falling away** from the living God. But encourage one another day after day, as long as it is still called "Today," lest anyone of you be hardened by the deceitfulness of sin. For we have become partakers of Christ, **if we hold fast the beginning of our assurance firm until the end…**"
>
> Colossians 1:22-23 "…He has now reconciled you in His fleshly body through death, in order to present you before Him holy and blameless and beyond reproach-if indeed you continue in the faith firmly established and steadfast, and not moved away from the hope of the gospel that you have heard, which was proclaimed in all creation under heaven, and of which I, Paul, was made a minister."

There is a small word that is common to both passages. That word is 'if.' It is small, but so very important. Our salvation is conditional. We will gain salvation only **if** we hold on to our faith. We have a healthy hope for salvation because we are motivated to be faithful until the end of our lives. This does not discourage me. My hope grows stronger every day, and my desire to abide in Jesus is renewed each day. My salvation may not be assured, but it is getting closer with each passing day, as Paul reminded the believers in Rome. "...for now salvation is **nearer** to us than when we believed."(Romans 13:11)

Indeed, the Bible teaches that we have an assurance of hope. However the Bible does not teach that we have an assurance of salvation. Unfortunately, the 'assurance of salvation' doctrine is taught in many churches today. In the next section I will discuss the danger of what I call 'assurance teaching.'

The Danger of Assurance Teaching

To understand the danger of 'assurance teaching' we need to first look at the early church. The early church was heavily persecuted, both by the Jews and more severely by the Romans. During one period it was a crime to be a Christian. People were persecuted and put to death for being Christians. Here's how the book of Hebrews describes their plight.

> Hebrews 11:36-38 "...others experienced mockings and scourgings, yes, also chains and imprisonment. They were stoned, they were sawn in two, they were tempted, they were put to death with the sword; they went about in sheepskins, in goatskins, being destitute, afflicted, ill-treated, wandering in deserts and mountains and caves and holes in the ground."

Many of these could have escaped their plight by renouncing their belief in Jesus; but they chose to remain faithful to Jesus, even unto death. Why did they do that? Because their faith in an afterlife with Jesus was strong, and they did not want to lose out on their salvation. They clearly understood that they had to be prepared to lose their lives for their faith. **They also understood that they could be disqualified from entering the Kingdom of God if they renounced their faith to prolong their life on earth.**

You may be wondering why I am talking about the persecution of the early church. It is simply because I believe true believers will face similar persecutions in the 'end times.' A time is coming which the Bible calls the 'great tribulation.' During this period of time it will be very risky to truly believe in Jesus Christ, to be a genuine Christian. And yes, the church will be around for the 'great tribulation.'

Many churches teach that the Church will be taken out of the world or 'Raptured' prior to the 'great tribulation.' There is even a best-selling series of books in circulation that supports this notion. However the book of Revelation indicates that true believers will still be around; and they will be persecuted and put to death. Look at the following passages.

> Revelation 6:11 "…they were told that they should rest for a little while longer, until the number of their fellow servants and their brethren who were to be killed even as they had been, should be completed also."
>
> Revelation 20:4-5 "And I saw the souls of those who had been beheaded because of the testimony of Jesus and because of the word of God, and those who had not worshiped the beast or his image, and had not received the mark upon their forehead and

upon their hand; and they came to life and reigned with Christ for a thousand years. The rest of the dead did not come to life until the thousand years were completed."

So what does all of this have to do with 'assurance teaching?' Imagine the following scenario. A Christian who has been convinced that his or her salvation is assured finds himself or herself in the 'great tribulation' period. During that period there will be a person the Bible calls 'the beast' who will demand to be worshipped and obeyed. Evidence of that allegiance will be something the Bible calls the 'mark of the beast' to be placed on each person's forehead or hand. If a person refuses the 'mark' he or she will be unable to buy or sell anything. Now, a person with an assurance mindset may think, 'I won't lose my salvation if I take the mark because my salvation is assured. I may lose a couple of rewards in heaven, but at least I will get in. I don't want to finish my time here on earth in poverty. God will understand.' However look at what the Bible says.

> Revelation 14:9-12 "**If anyone worships the beast and his image, and receives a mark on his forehead or upon his hand, he also will drink of the wine of the wrath of God**, which is mixed in full strength in the cup of His anger; and he will be tormented with fire and brimstone in the presence of the holy angels and in the presence of the Lamb. And **the smoke of their torment goes up forever and ever**; and they have no rest day and night, those who worship the beast and his image, and whoever receives the mark of his name. Here is the perseverance of the saints who keep the commandments of God and their faith in Jesus."

The Bible is quite clear. If you take the 'mark of the beast', you will go to hell-no exceptions. Now let's look at the same scenario, but with a true believer who has a 'hopeful' mindset. That person will refuse to take the 'mark of the beast,' because he or she knows they must persevere in faith until the end of their lives to gain salvation. They know the Bible tells them not to take the mark; and they will obey Jesus Christ, even if it means poverty, even if it means death. In losing their lives here on earth, they will gain their lives in heaven.

So then in a nutshell, **'assurance teaching' is dangerous because it diminishes a person's motivation to persevere in the faith** when the going gets really tough. On the other hand, **a person with a 'hopeful' mindset will be quite motivated to persevere in the faith, because they know their very salvation is at risk by the decisions they make.**

The Bible tells us that God is just, and that people will be without excuse by the decisions they freely make in their lives. The Bible teaches us that in the end times, God will allow powerful delusions to draw people away from obeying Him, so that He may rightly discern between those that are His and those that are not His. Deception is a real stumbling block for many today and will become even more so as the end times draw near. In the next section I will discuss deception in this world.

Deception

The dictionary defines deception as the act of making a person or persons believe as true something that is false. Deceit is further defined as concealing or twisting the truth in order to mislead or gain advantage over others.

To mislead is to cause a person or persons to follow the wrong course or to err in conduct or action. The first thing to understand, as we discuss deception in the world, is that deception is one of the main weapons if not **the** main weapon that Satan uses against us. At this point it would be prudent for us to discuss Satan and his ploys. As in any warfare one must understand one's enemy in order to build an effective defense.

The Bible has much to say about Satan. One of the most important things the Bible teaches us is that Satan is the spiritual ruler of this world. (Luke 4:6) For some reason in ages past, Satan, one of God's created angels, rebelled against God and was defeated. Satan and the angels that followed him were cast from heaven to the Earth, and it is here that they reside. The angels that followed Satan are sometimes called 'fallen angels.' They are also called 'demons.' You might be wondering why God didn't just destroy Satan and his demons, and why did God grant Satan the Earth to rule? My belief is that God has used and will continue to use Satan and his demons as instruments to separate out the 'wheat from the chaff,' as the Bible characterizes 'believers and non-believers.' Let's look at some Bible passages that support what I have asserted in this paragraph.

> Luke 4:5-6 "And he led Him up and showed Him all the kingdoms of the world in a moment of time. And the devil said to Him, "I will give You all this domain and its glory; **for it has been handed over to me** and I give it to whomever I wish."" (Satan tempting Jesus)
>
> Revelation 12:9 "And the great dragon was thrown down, the serpent of old who is called the **devil**

> **and Satan, who deceives the whole world**; he was thrown down to the earth, and his angels were thrown down with him."
>
> Luke 10:18 "And He said to them, "I was watching Satan fall from heaven like lightening."(Jesus speaking with His disciples)

Jesus knew all about Satan and his deceptive nature. In fact, Jesus characterized Satan as a liar. Here's how Jesus described Satan.

> John 8:44 "He was a murderer from the beginning, and does not stand in the truth, because **there is no truth in him**. Whenever he speaks a lie, he speaks from his own nature; for **he is a liar, and the father of lies**."

Now, combine the propensity to lie with supernatural powers and the desire to destroy God's creation, and you have a challenging situation for mankind. Satan's goal is to turn people away from the truth, and in so doing, cause their eternal destruction. Look at what the apostle Peter said about Satan.

> 1 Peter 5:8 "Be of sober spirit, be on the alert. Your adversary, the devil, prowls about like a roaring lion, seeking someone to devour."

Why would God allow Satan to be such a destructive force in the world? The Bible teaches us that God allows the deception to occur in order to separate true believers from non-believers. God is just, and in the final judgment people will be fairly judged on the choices they personally made. If they believe in The Truth, Jesus Christ, they will not be deceived by Satan and his demons. However if they reject The Truth, they will be easily deceived. The following passage is quite telling in this regard.

> 2 Thessalonians 2:8-12 "And then that lawless one will be revealed whom the Lord will slay with the breath of His mouth and bring to an end by the appearance of His coming; that is, the one whose coming is in accord with the activity of Satan, with all the power and signs and false wonders, and with all the deception of wickedness for those who perish, because they did not receive the love of the truth, so as to be saved. And for this reason **God will send upon them a deluding influence so that they might believe what is false, in order that they all may be judged who did not believe the truth but took pleasure in wickedness.**"

You might be wondering at this point, 'What does deception look like? How can I know what is true and what is false?' There is only one way to know what is true, and that is to test everything by what the Bible says. Deception is so effective because it seems right, looks right, feels right, and we want it to be right. However if the Bible doesn't support that which seems right, looks right, feels right, or what we want to be right; it is deception. Look at this next passage.

> Proverbs 14:12 "There is a way which seems right to a man, but its end is the way of death."

We cannot trust in our senses to guide us down the right path. Being a pilot I like to use the analogy of instrument flying. If I fly my airplane into the clouds and rely on my senses to keep me upright, the airplane will soon be in a dangerous attitude. I may well be upside down and think that I am right side up. I must force myself to rely on my instruments to control the airplane. There is a phenomenon called the 'leans' where a pilot, flying between cloud layers, which are not parallel with the ground, feels like he is flying in a banked or leaned attitude when his instruments tell him he is level. He must force himself to trust the instruments, which are accurate. His senses are not. **The Bible is like an airplane's instruments. It tells us what is right or true when our feelings disagree.**

Satan uses many things in this world to deceive the masses. He uses the news media, movies, TV, books, schools, our associates and the workplace to name a few. However I believe he has done his most effective and devastatingly deceptive work in religion. Whenever and wherever religion has taken away from or added to the Bible, it has deceived the masses. Several religions use the Bible in a limited way. However they have added their own doctrines and/or beliefs that are sometimes contrary to what the Bible teaches. Then they tell the masses that the leaders of the religion are the only ones who can correctly interpret the Bible. If their religious doctrine conflicts with the Bible, the doctrine takes precedence.

The apostle Paul warned early believers of deception entering the church. He told them to watch out for church leaders who would introduce false doctrine, while appearing to be true and righteous people. Here's what Paul said to the early church in Corinth.

> 2 Corinthians 11:13-15 "For such men are false apostles, deceitful workers, disguising themselves as apostles of Christ. And no wonder, for even Satan disguises himself as an angel of light. Therefore

it is not surprising if his servants also disguise themselves as servants of righteousness; whose end shall be according to their deeds."

Our only hope against deception is to be so firmly anchored in the Bible, The Word of God, that when a lie occurs it is immediately detected. One very good example of a contemporary deception is the book, 'The Da Vinci Code.' It has become very popular with the masses with the notion that Jesus was married to Mary Magdalene and they had children. However if one is firmly anchored in the Bible, the deception becomes obvious. The Bible teaches that with the exception of Jesus, all of mankind has been infected with a sinful nature. This sinful nature is passed from generation to generation. Jesus was sin-free, because His mother, Mary, was impregnated by the Holy Spirit of God. Jesus had to be free of sin in order to be the perfect sacrifice and atone for the sins of mankind. There would be no requirement for additional sin-free offspring, as God's purpose was fulfilled completely in Jesus. Furthermore, 'The Da Vinci Code' has the effect of 'adding to the Bible,' which is specifically forbidden in the Bible, as the following passage indicates.

> Revelation 22:18-19 "I testify to everyone who hears the words of the prophecy of this book: if anyone adds to them, God shall add to him the plagues which are written in this book; and if anyone takes away from the words of the book of this prophecy, God shall take away his part from the tree of life and from the holy city, which are written in this book."

Another recent deception attempt was the reintroduction of 'The Gospel of Judas,' which was rejected by the early church. National Geographic and the news media made this 'discovery' a big deal. The 'gospel' suggests that Jesus made a deal with Judas to betray Jesus. Judas wasn't such a bad guy, the 'gospel' proclaims. Again, it is exposed as a lie if one is firmly rooted in the Bible. It conflicts with the rest of the Bible, and it has the effect of adding to the Bible. One very good example of this gospel's conflict with the Bible is found in the book of John, as Jesus prayed to God the Father.

> John 17:12 "While I was with them, I was keeping them in Thy name which Thou hast given Me; and I guarded them, and not one of them perished but the son of perdition, that the Scripture might be fulfilled."

If Jesus described Judas as 'the son of perdition,' it is doubtful that Jesus and Judas together orchestrated Jesus' crucifixion. The 'Gospel of Judas' was rightly rejected by the early church as a lie.

Another type of deception is 'self-deception.' This is when we try to convince ourselves that something is true or right when in fact it is wrong. Let me illustrate self-deception with an example. Suppose that I am a married man. Suppose, also, that my marriage is going through some difficulties, and my relationship with my wife is strained. Suppose that by some 'quirk of fate' that I 'happen across' an old girlfriend, and we strike up a conversation. Old feelings toward this girlfriend resurface, and I find out she is a stronger Christian than I perceive my wife to be. In fact, I perceive that she is a 'real believer,' and my wife isn't. Now, I know that the Bible says that a divorce is OK if a 'non-believing' spouse leaves a 'believing' spouse. So, I stop trying to fix the problems in my marriage, hoping that my wife will leave me so that I can go to my old girlfriend. I have stopped 'loving my wife as Christ loves the church.' I have deceived myself into doing the wrong thing. I have deceived myself into thinking that God will approve of this course of action. I even think that God has brought my old girlfriend into my life again.

I know a person who actually did this and deceived himself right into a divorce. His wife knew about his renewed relationship with an old girlfriend and filed for a divorce. He didn't try to stop it. In fact it was all going according to his self-deceived plan. He continued in his self-deception until two things happened: 1) He heard a radio Bible teacher teach about a 'believing' husband subtly forcing a 'non-believing' wife to leave. 2.) One of his sons said to him that he was not demonstrating the Biblical model of 'loving his wife as Christ loved the Church.'

It was enough to make him realize the error of his ways. He confessed his sin to God and promised with God's help to change his ways. He begged God to let him win his wife back, and promised to love her as God said in His Word. They were remarried one year after the divorce, and their second marriage is far better than the first marriage.

I believe that deception will be the number one stumbling block preventing many from reaching salvation. The Bible predicts that deception will turn people away from their faith. Look at the following passage.

> 1 Timothy 4:1 "But the Spirit explicitly says that in later times **some will <u>fall away</u> from the faith**, paying attention to deceitful spirits and doctrines of demons…"

This is another reason that 'assurance teaching' is so dangerous. Many will be deceived into thinking their salvation is assured. In my opinion these people will be more susceptible to slight variations of the Truth and be less likely to test everything in light of Scripture. Furthermore if they wrongly interpreted Scripture to conclude their salvation is assured, they will most likely continue to wrongly interpret God's Truth. The following passage may well apply to the 'assurance' crowd.

> Obadiah 1:3 "The arrogance of your heart has deceived you..."

With regard to the Truth, we must not trust others. We must not even trust ourselves. There is only one source of Truth-The Word of God, the Bible. We are in a spiritual battle for our very souls. We cannot see our enemy, because our battle is against the spiritual world. Because we are in a very real battle and our eternity is at stake, we must arm ourselves effectively. Again, the Bible tells us what to do. We have already seen this passage, but we need to look at it again.

> Ephesians 6:10-18 "Finally, be strong in the Lord, and in the strength of His might. **Put on the full armor of God, that you may be able to stand firm against the schemes of the devil.** For our struggle is not against flesh and blood, but against the rulers, against the powers, against the world forces of this darkness, against the spiritual forces of wickedness in the heavenly places. Therefore, **take up the full armor of God, that you may be able to resist in the evil day, and having done everything, to stand firm.** Stand firm therefore, having girded your loins

with **truth,** and having put on the **breastplate of righteousness,** and having shod your feet with the **preparation of the gospel of peace**; in addition to all, taking up the **shield of faith** with which you will be able to extinguish all the flaming missiles of the evil one. And take the **helmet of salvation,** and the **sword of the Spirit**, which is the word of God. With all prayer and petition pray at all times in the Spirit, and with this in view, **be on the alert with all perseverance…**"

The Bible is integral to each article in the 'full armor of God.' First of all, the Bible is the Truth. Secondly, one can only understand 'righteousness' by reading the Bible. Thirdly, the 'gospel of peace' is defined only in the Bible. Fourth, the faith that is required is faith in Jesus Christ, who is the living Word of God. Fifth, the pathway to salvation is only defined in the Bible. Finally, the 'sword of the spirit' is the Word of God, the Bible. I therefore conclude that one must be immersed in the Bible to effectively fight against deception. It is the only way. Deception is so powerful. Let's look at this final passage to wrap up this section.

> Matthew 24:24 "For false Christs and false prophets will arise and will show great signs and wonders, so as to mislead, if possible, even the elect."

Even God's elect will be challenged to cling to the truth and not be deceived. Remember, deception will look, feel and seem so right; and the Bible may seem wrong. However, like the pilot who trusts his instruments even when his senses tell him otherwise, we must trust the Bible. Otherwise we will 'crash.' In the next section we will look more closely at God's elect.

God's Elect

Thus far we have examined the pathway to salvation and the paths that lead away from salvation. We have also discussed the notion that no person is assured of his or her salvation. Only God knows who will make it into heaven. These fortunate souls are called 'the elect.' These are the persons who will persevere in their active belief in Jesus Christ and not 'fall away.' While we cannot know for certain if we are one of God's elect, we can and should look at what the Bible says in regard to God's elect. We will then be better able to examine ourselves to see if we are 'in the faith.' First of all, the Bible confirms that nobody knows who are of God's elect. Look at the following passage.

> Romans 8:19 "For the anxious longing of the creation **waits eagerly for the revealing of the sons of God**."

All of creation is waiting to see God's elect, those God has specifically chosen for salvation. The Bible is clear. Those destined for heaven have been chosen by God for that purpose. The following Bible passages confirm this.

> Romans 8:29-30 "For **whom He foreknew, He also predestined to become conformed to the image of His Son**, that He might be the first-born among many brethren; and whom He predestined, these He also called; and whom He called, these He also justified; and whom He justified, these He also glorified."
>
> Romans 9:18 "So then **He has mercy on whom He desires, and He hardens whom He desires**."

So then, it appears that God's elect are those who at some point in their lives are 'called' by God. To what are they called? They are called to believe in Jesus Christ; and in the process of believing in Jesus they are transformed, sanctified and conformed to the image of Jesus. Those who persevere in their transformation are then chosen by God for salvation. However not all who are 'called' are 'chosen' as the following passage indicates.

> Matthew 22:11-14 "…he saw there a man not dressed in wedding clothes, and he said to him, 'Friend, how did you come in here without wedding clothes?' And he was speechless. Then the king said to the servants, 'Bind him hand and foot, and cast him into the outer darkness; in that place there shall be weeping and gnashing of teeth.' **For many are called, but few are chosen.**"

We must be 'called' and 'chosen' to be selected for salvation. We must remain faithful until our death in order to be saved. Look at the following passage, which describes those who are 'called,' 'chosen' and 'faithful'-those who belong to Jesus Christ.

> Revelation 17:14 "… He is Lord of lords and King of kings, and **those who are with Him are the called and chosen and faithful.**"

I believe we can definitely know if we have been called to believe in Jesus Christ. What we cannot know is if we will be chosen for salvation. While we are faithful to our calling, we will enjoy the spiritual benefits of believing in Jesus. We will have the Holy Spirit within us and enjoy the fruits of the Holy Spirit. We will have what the Bible calls eternal life, 'knowing Jesus.' What we do not know is if we will persevere in our faith until the end of our lives. We don't know what trials lie ahead.

Charles Darwin is a good example of a professed Christian turning away from his faith. He was a professed Christian until his ten-year old daughter died. Her death caused Charles Darwin to stop believing in God. He was angry that God would allow his daughter to die. He couldn't believe that a loving God would allow that to happen. Charles Darwin turned away from Christianity, and the result was the 'Theory of Evolution.' Charles Darwin failed a crucial test of his faith. I seriously doubt Charles Darwin was one of God's elect. He might have been called into the Christian faith, but most likely was not chosen for salvation. However, I don't know what will happen to Charles Darwin in eternity. Only God knows the fate of Charles Darwin. One thing is certain, though. Charles Darwin no longer believes in evolution.

Characteristics Of God's Elect

While we may not know if we will be chosen, it is useful to examine some of the characteristics of those who are on the right track. Again, the Bible is not silent on these important characteristics. First of all, **those headed toward salvation will have and exhibit a hunger for and an understanding of the Word of God, the Bible.** Here are some passages that support this.

> 1 Corinthians 1:18 "For the word of the cross is to those who are perishing foolishness, but to us who are **being saved** it is the power of God."
>
> Psalm 40:8 "**I delight to do Thy will, O my God.** Thy law is within my heart."

> Isaiah 66:2 "But to this one I will look, **to him who is humble and contrite of spirit, and who trembles at My word.**"

Not only do those being saved want to read and understand the Bible, they want to obey what the Bible tells them to do. In other words **they want to live by faith**. We have already seen some of the following passages, but they need to be examined in light of defining those who are headed for salvation. Let's look.

> Romans 1:16-17 "For I am not ashamed of the gospel, for it is the power of God for salvation to everyone who believes, to the Jew first and also to the Greek. For in it **the righteousness of God is revealed from faith to faith**; as it is written, "But the righteous man shall live by faith.""

> Habakkuk 2:4 "Behold, as for the proud one, his soul is not right within him; but **the righteous will live by his faith.**"

As a result of living by faith, the Bible teaches us that **the elect will suffer hardships along the way**. A believer's faith will indeed be tested to determine if it is genuine. Some will pass, and some will fail their tests. Remember Darwin? If a person does not experience hardships along the way, perhaps that person is right where Satan wants him or her to be. Let's examine what the Bible says about suffering and trials for the believer.

> Philippians 1:29 "For to you it has been granted for Christ's sake, not only to believe in Him, but also to suffer for His sake..."

> Hebrews 12:6 "...for those whom the Lord loves He disciplines, and He scourges every son whom He receives."
>
> Psalm 34:19 "Many are the afflictions of the righteous; but the Lord delivers him out of them all."

Another revealing trait of the elect is the way in which they view and handle money. **God's elect are not focused on wealth and money**. They may be wealthy, but they do not set their hearts on money. They are generous with their wealth, giving and lending freely. They do not worry about money, trusting in God to provide for them. Here's what the Bible says in this regard.

> Matthew 6:24 "No one can serve two masters; for either he will hate the one and love the other, or he will hold to one and despise the other. **You cannot serve God and mammon.**"
>
> Psalm 37:21 "The wicked borrows and does not pay back, but **the righteous is gracious and gives.**"

Another characteristic of the elect is that they possess one or more spiritual gifts. I won't list all of the spiritual gifts, but an excellent Biblical reference is 1 Corinthians 12. Spiritual gifts are skills or talents that the Holy Spirit bestows upon believers. These gifts are given to each believer for the benefit of the entire church. Gifts include teaching skills, Biblical interpretation, extra faith, wisdom, encouraging others, leadership, helping others, giving, just to name a few. There are others. If one is a believer, he or she will be aware of the gift or gifts they possess. They will also use their gifts for the benefit of other believers.

Bearing Fruit

Another very important characteristic or indication of one's true belief are the <u>results</u> of their thoughts, words and deeds. In other words, as the Bible puts it, is the fruit of their lives good or bad? The difficulty, here, is that none of us is very good at inspecting fruit. This is because a right action sometimes produces temporary hardships before something wonderful is realized. We may look at the temporary hardship and call it bad fruit. I want to share an example of this happening in my family.

My daughter was going through a difficult time in her life and was in bondage to drug use. She was depressed and at times suicidal. She had very little hope for her future and didn't want to go on. In the middle of her mess, she decided to put her trust in God. It was slow going at first, but her faith was genuine. In fact, her drug challenges seemed to intensify after she chose to trust in God.

At a family gathering my daughter and my older brother engaged in a conversation about God, faith, and her belief in the Bible. My daughter argued for belief in the Bible, and my brother argued against the Bible. As the debate intensified, my brother suggested that my daughter's beliefs had not benefited her, referring to her drug problem and loneliness. In other words, my brother perceived my daughter's faith had produced bad fruit in her life. However my daughter persisted in her faith.

Moving ahead several years, my daughter has a beautiful, normal and healthy daughter: our first grandchild. She is also pursuing a successful career with a major department store chain. Her faith is stronger than ever, and she has a wonderful hope for the future. I conclude her faith in God and her belief in God's Word, the Bible, has produced very good fruit in her life. We must not be too hasty with our 'fruit inspection.' Let's look at what the Bible says about bearing fruit as evidence of one's belief.

> Luke 6:43-45 "For there is no good tree which produces bad fruit; nor, on the other hand, a bad tree which produces good fruit. For each tree is known by its own fruit. For men do not gather figs from thorns, nor do they pick grapes from a briar bush. The good man out of the good treasure of his heart brings forth what is good; and the evil man out of the evil treasure brings forth what is evil; **for his mouth speaks from that which fills his heart.**" (Jesus speaking)
>
> John 15:4-8 "Abide in Me, and I in you. As the branch cannot bear fruit of itself, unless it abides in the vine, so neither can you, unless you abide in Me. I am the vine, you are the branches; **he who abides in Me, and I in him, he bears much fruit**; for apart from Me you can do nothing. If anyone does not abide in Me, he is thrown away as a branch, and dries up; and they gather them, and cast them into the fire, and they are burned. If you abide in Me, and My words abide in you, ask whatever you wish, and it shall be done for you. By this is My father glorified, **that you bear much fruit, and so <u>prove</u> to be My disciples.**" (Jesus speaking)

So then, bearing good fruit in one's life is mandatory. God is clear. If we aren't bearing good fruit in our lives, we are not of God's elect. If we don't have a genuine love for the Word of God, we are not of God's elect. If we love money more than God, we are not of God's elect. If we don't live by faith, we are not of God's elect. The Bible lists other indicators of true belief, and I leave it to you to find them. However we have enough information to see if we truly are believers. The apostle Paul told the church members in Corinth, "Test yourselves to see if you are in the faith; examine yourselves!"(2 Corinthians 13:5)

Before we leave this section regarding God's elect, we need to discuss one other thing. We need to realize that a life of faith is a transforming process. Also, people are called into the faith at different points in their lives. Some are called early and some are called late. The point here is that one mould doesn't fit all. A person may be one of God's elect, but has not yet been called. Prior to their calling they would in all likelihood not demonstrate any of the characteristics of a true believer. So, we cannot really conclude that a person is not of God's elect if they don't yet exhibit any of the previously mentioned characteristics. However after a person professes belief and chooses to make Jesus Christ Lord of their life, the transformation or sanctification process should make these characteristics become evident, providing a gauge for the believer to measure himself or herself against.

In the next section I want to address what I call the 'assurance passages.' I want to discuss the passages that indicate to many Christians that they can know that they will go to heaven- the passages that seem to give an assurance of salvation.

The Assurance Passages

Before I deal with specific 'assurance passages,' it would be useful to revisit the Biblical definition of 'eternal life.'

Eternal life is the life that is enjoyed through an active belief and knowledge of Jesus Christ. Jesus defined it quite clearly in John 17:3. "And **this is eternal life, that they may know Thee, the only true God, and Jesus Christ whom Thou hast sent**." The choice of the word 'eternal' is somewhat puzzling, because the Bible demonstrates that one can fall away from an active relationship with Jesus Christ. That person would no longer know Jesus and, by definition, would no longer have 'eternal life.' Many of the 'assurance passages' refer to believers knowing they have life. However through their own choices, they may lose it prior to their physical death. Now, let's look at some of those 'assurance passages.'

> 1 John 3:14 "We know that we have passed **out of death into life**, because we love the brethren."
>
> 1 John 5:13 "These things I have written to you who believe in the name of the Son of God, **in order that you may know that you have eternal life**."
>
> John 5:24 "Truly, truly, I say to you, **he who hears My word, and believes Him who sent Me has eternal life**, and does not come into judgment, but has passed out of death into life."

All of these passages refer to eternal life as defined in the Bible. These people can know they have life. What they cannot know is if they will someday choose to reject their faith and depart from that life. **Eternal life depends on an active belief in Jesus Christ**. It is **contingent** on an active and real faith. The author of the book of Hebrews realized this and communicated his concerns to the early church. Look at what he wrote.

> Hebrews 3:12-14 "Take care, brethren, lest there should be in an one of you an evil, unbelieving heart, in **falling away** from the living God. But encourage one another day after day, as long as it is still called "Today," lest any one of you be hardened by the deceitfulness of sin. For we have become partakers of Christ, **if** we hold fast the beginning of our assurance firm until the end..."

Nothing could be clearer. 'We have become partakers of Christ, **if** we hold fast the beginning of our assurance firm until the end.' The author wasn't talking about 'assurance of salvation.' Rather, he was speaking about the 'assurance of hope.' Look at this next passage.

> Hebrews 6:11 "And we desire that each one of you show the same diligence so as to realize the full **assurance of hope** until the end..."

The Apostle Peter also realized that a person's salvation was conditional on an active and true faith until death. Let's look at what Peter said.

> 2 Peter 1:10-11 "Therefore, brethren, **be all the more diligent to make certain about His calling and choosing you**; for as long as you practice these things you will never stumble; for in this way the entrance into the eternal kingdom of our Lord and Savior Jesus Christ will be abundantly supplied to you."

Both Peter and Paul, who knew Jesus more personally than any of us, did not subscribe to the notion that their salvation was assured. They knew that even they had to persevere in their faith until they died. They knew that they could only maintain a healthy hope for their salvation. Paul's letters to the Romans and the Philippians support this.

> Romans 8:23-25 "And not only this, but also we ourselves, having the first fruits of the Spirit, even we ourselves groan within ourselves, waiting eagerly for our adoption as sons, the redemption of our body. **For in hope we have been saved, but hope that is seen is not hope; for why does one also hope for what he sees? But if we hope for what we do not see, with perseverance we wait eagerly for it.**"

> Philippians 3:11-14 "...in order that I may attain to the resurrection from the dead. **Not that I have already obtained it, or have already become perfect, but I press on in order that I may lay hold of that for which also I was laid hold of by Christ Jesus. Brethren, I do not regard myself as having laid hold of it yet; but one thing I do: forgetting what lies behind and reaching forward to what lies ahead, I press on toward the goal for the prize of the upward call of God in Christ Jesus.**"

Paul also realized that his preaching to others would not assure his own salvation. He realized that after teaching others the way to salvation, there was still a potential even for him to fall away; so he consciously guarded against that possibility. Look at what he said.

> 1 Corinthians 9:27 "...but I buffet my body and make it my slave, lest possibly, after I have preached to others, I myself should be disqualified."

Let's examine two more 'assurance passages.' These passages spoken by Jesus imply that He will not reject anyone that comes to Him.

> John 6:37 "**All that the Father gives Me shall come to Me,** and the one who comes to Me I will certainly not cast out."
>
> John 6:39-40 "…of all that He has given Me, I lose nothing, but raise it up on the last day. For this is the will of My Father, **that everyone who beholds the Son and believes in Him, may have eternal life; and I Myself will raise him up on the last day.**"

While it is true that Jesus will not cast out or lose believers who have come to him, it is also true that the believer can choose to depart from an active belief or faith in Jesus Christ. Our freedom of choice does not depart from us at the moment we believe in Jesus. We still have the freedom to choose between right and wrong, good and evil, and truth and deception. There still remains a need to persevere in one's belief. However as long as we remain faithful to the Word of God, persevering in our faith when the going gets tough, Jesus will not cast us away from Him. This next passage is one that the 'assurance teachers' use to suggest that even the believer cannot separate himself or herself from Jesus.

> Romans 8:38-39 "For I am convinced that neither death, nor life, nor angels, nor principalities, nor things present, nor things to come, nor powers, nor height, nor depth, nor any other created thing, shall be able to separate us from the love of God, which is in Christ Jesus our Lord."

The 'assurance teachers' focus on the phase 'any other created thing' and proclaim that the believer himself fits into that grouping. However that interpretation doesn't harmonize with the rest of the Bible. Let's revisit a couple of passages that would conflict with this interpretation.

> Hebrews 3:12-14 "Take care, brethren, lest there should be in an one of you an evil, unbelieving heart, in **falling away** from the living God. But encourage one another day after day, as long as it is still called "Today," lest any one of you be hardened by the deceitfulness of sin. For we have become partakers of Christ, <u>if</u> **we hold fast the beginning of our assurance firm until the end…**"
>
> 1 Timothy 4:1 "But the Spirit explicitly says that in later times **some will <u>fall away</u> from the faith**, paying attention to deceitful spirits and doctrines of demons."

A more accurate interpretation of the 'Romans' passage would be that as long as a believer perseveres in true faith, God prevents anything or anybody from taking away that faith. Again, it is conditional on the person persevering in his or her faith in Jesus Christ. The person always has the choice of departing from or remaining in the faith. God's elect will not depart from their faith.

These next 'assurance passages' are also **conditional** on a continued and active belief in Jesus Christ. Notice the phrases 'shall be saved' and 'shall live' indicating a future event.

> Romans 10:9-13 "…if you confess with your mouth Jesus as Lord, and believe in your heart that God raised Him from the dead, you **<u>shall be saved</u>**; for with the heart man believes, resulting in righteousness, and with the mouth he confesses, **resulting in salvation**. For the Scripture says,

> "Whoever believes in Him will not be disappointed." For there is no distinction between Jew and Greek; for the same Lord is Lord of all, abounding in riches for all who call upon Him; for "Whoever will call upon the name of the Lord will be saved.""
>
> John 11:25-26 "Jesus said to her, "I am the resurrection and the life; **he who believes in Me shall live** even if he dies, and everyone who lives and believes in Me shall never die."

This next passage is one the 'assurance teachers' lean upon heavily. They are confident that Jesus will bring them to salvation no matter what happens. Again, I maintain that the Bible teaches a requirement for the person to sustain an active belief or faith in the living Word of God, Jesus Christ, to reach salvation. Let's look at the passage.

> Philippians 1:6 "For I am confident of this very thing, that **He who began a good work in you will perfect it until the day of Christ Jesus.**"

Yes, Jesus will continue to transform us **if** we continue in the faith. We all need help in our journey of Faith, for the pathway to salvation is filled with challenges. When we fall off the pathway **and are truly sorry**, God will help us to resume our journey. Let's look at another often-used 'assurance passage.'

> 1 John 3:14 "We know that we have passed out of death into life, because we love the brethren."

With regard to this passage, two points need to be addressed. First, the life that is mentioned is the life that is dependent on a present belief in Jesus. This life has a present value. It also has a future value, if the person continues in his or her belief. If the person departs from believing in Jesus, he or she loses their spiritual life. The second point involves the meaning of 'loving the brethren.' What does that mean? Let's look at the Bible for an accurate assessment of 'loving the brethren.'

1 John 5:2 **"By this we know that we love the children of God, <u>when we love God and observe His commandments.</u>"**

OK. How many of us perfectly keep God's commandments? I would say approximately none. Then how do we know that we 'love the brethren?' I will admit that those who believe in Jesus Christ and know that the Bible is the truth have a special kinship or bond. It is easy to converse with like-minded people, and we like being around them. Is that 'loving the brethren?' What if one of the 'brethren' asked us for money or some other support? How would 'loving the brethren' look then?

When we look at the 'assurance passages' we see that for the most part they speak of the believer knowing he or she has 'life.' As I mentioned at the beginning of this section, we must use the Biblical definition of life. We cannot rely on our flawed human logic for it is flawed. The Bible is quite clear that we only have spiritual life when we abide in Jesus through our active faith in the Word of God. The Bible is also clear that we have the ability to depart from an active Faith in Jesus Christ who is the living Word of God. If we choose to depart from our Faith in Jesus Christ, we will lose our Spiritual Life. If we die in that state, we will in all likelihood not gain salvation.

We cannot be assured of our salvation, but we can know when we have an active and real faith in Jesus Christ. **We must persevere in our active faith and hope that we will gain salvation when we die.** In the next section I will address what I call the 'hopeful passages.'

The Hopeful Passages

Let me first say that hope is a good thing. While Hope is not assurance, it is almost assurance. One could say, perhaps, that hope is 90% assurance. **The crucial difference between hope and assurance is that hope necessitates perseverance. Assurance does not.** In fact, assurance relaxes perseverance.

Hope is a crucial mindset in resisting temptation, in being obedient to the Word of God. A hopeful mindset is also essential in knowing Jesus and having eternal life. With an assurance mindset we are not as motivated to persevere in obeying the Word of God. Therefore, I believe, those with an assurance mindset are at greater risk for departing from God.

The apostle Paul didn't rest in any assurance of gaining salvation. He believed he would gain salvation only if he persevered in his faith. Look again at what he wrote to the Roman church.

> Romans 8:23-25 "And not only this, but also we ourselves, having the first fruits of the Spirit, even we ourselves groan within ourselves, waiting eagerly for our adoption as sons, the redemption of our body. **For in hope we have been saved, but hope that is seen is not hope; for why does one also hope for what he sees? But if we hope for what we do not see, with perseverance we wait eagerly for it.**"

We can see clearly from this passage that Paul was eagerly waiting for his salvation. He believed he would make it. However he was not arrogant or presumptuous in his belief. He knew there still remained trials for him to face. He knew that he was capable of failing trials and would have to maintain an active faith in Jesus Christ in difficult times. In short, he knew the only way to salvation was to persevere in his faith. Let's look at another 'hopeful passage.'

> Colossians 1:22-23 "…He has now reconciled you in His fleshly body through death, in order to present you before Him holy and blameless and beyond reproach-**if indeed you continue in the faith firmly established and steadfast, and not moved away from the <u>hope</u> of the gospel** that you have heard, which was proclaimed in all creation under heaven, and of which I, Paul, was made a minister."

This passage confirms that our salvation is conditional on our continuing in the faith. It also supports that the gospel of Jesus Christ gives us hope for our salvation, rather than an assurance of our salvation. Here's another 'hopeful' passage that underlines the conditional nature of our salvation.

> Hebrews 3:6 "…but Christ was faithful as a Son over His house whose house we are, **if we hold fast our confidence and the boast of our hope firm until the end…**"

It's pretty clear that we need to cling to our hope of salvation and demonstrate our faith until the end of our lives. This next 'hopeful passage' indicates that Paul believed he would gain salvation, but he uses the word 'might' to indicate that it was not a 'done deal.'

Titus 3:4-7 "But when the kindness of God our Savior and His love for mankind appeared, He saved us, not on the basis of deeds which we have done in righteousness, but according to His mercy, by the washing of regeneration and renewing by the Holy Spirit, whom He poured out on us richly through Jesus Christ our Savior, that **being justified by His grace we <u>might</u> be made heirs according to the hope of eternal life.**"

Paul also tells us that we can be confident that a hopeful attitude will lead us to salvation. While we cannot have an assurance of salvation, we can have an assurance of hope. Look at this next passage.

Hebrews 6:11-12 "And we desire that each one of you show the same diligence so as to realize the **full assurance of hope until the end**, that you may **not be sluggish, but imitators of those who through faith and patience inherit the promises.**"

So then, how do we get and keep the hope that will lead us to salvation? As always, the Bible has the answer for us. Here it is.

Romans 5:3-5 "And not only this, but we also exult in our tribulations, knowing that **tribulation brings about perseverance; and perseverance, proven character; and proven character, hope; and hope does not disappoint,** because the love of God has been poured out within our hearts through the Holy Spirit who was given to us."

As we successfully navigate the trials in our lives by clinging to our faith, our character changes. Each trial teaches us how to persevere in our faith. Our character of faith grows stronger. Then, our hope for salvation is strengthened. As Paul says, the hope that we gain will not disappoint. In other words, **our genuine hope will lead us to salvation**. Indeed, it is a transforming process. We are transformed to be more like Jesus Christ as we persevere in our hope, as the following passage indicates.

> 1 John 3:3 "And everyone who has this **hope fixed on Him** purifies himself, just as He is pure."

However I want to again state that our hope is linked to our perseverance. There is hope as long as I desire to persevere in my faith. **When the desire to persevere is gone, hope is gone.** We therefore need to sustain our desire to persevere. To that end we need others to encourage us to persevere, as Paul told the church in Thessalonica.

> 1 Thessalonians 5:8-11 "But since we are of the day, let us be sober, having put on the breastplate of faith and love, and as a helmet, **the hope of salvation**. For God has not destined us for wrath, but for obtaining salvation through our Lord Jesus Christ, who died for us, that whether we are awake or asleep, we may live together with Him. **Therefore encourage one another, and build up one another**, just as you also are doing."

In this passage Paul again alludes to the spiritual battle we face by telling us implements of armor to wear. Notice that, **spiritually speaking, our vital parts are protected by faith, hope and love**. We must 'wear' them at all times, and the encouragement of other believers will help us to do so. Therefore we must find and associate with other believers for mutual encouragement. We may find them in a church. We may not. However, if we pray for them to come into our lives, God will send them to us.

I must digress and tell you a personal story about how God sent a believer into my life. A while back my son was moving his belongings from college to home in the family van. On the way home he was involved in an accident. He was very upset, and I tried to encourage him by saying God would make something good happen as a result of the accident.

Only a week prior to the accident, I had prayed for God to bring other believers into my life, so that I could have others with whom I could speak about the Bible. To make a long story short, the owner of the auto body shop where we had the van fixed has become my good friend and is a very dear brother in Jesus Christ. It was an expensive way to find a fellow believer, but well worth it.

At this point you should see that Scripture tells us to hope for our salvation and persevere in our faith in Jesus Christ. At no point does it say that we are assured of our salvation, no matter what we think, say, or do. On the contrary, the Bible teaches that as long as we live, we are all capable of turning away from an active belief in Jesus Christ. In fact, we are involved in a spiritual war in which Satan and his demons are actively trying to make us turn away from God. The forces of darkness are very powerful, and without God's help we stand little chance against them. Therefore, we must protect ourselves with God's spiritual armor. Furthermore, none of us can know if we will successfully persevere in our faith until we die. Only God knows those who will make it and gain salvation. Only God knows who are His elect. In the next section of this book I will reemphasize in more depth why a hopeful mindset is so important to our salvation.

Section III

WHY IS A HOPEFUL MINDSET SO IMPORTANT?

IN THIS SECTION I will demonstrate why having a 'hopeful' vs. 'assurance' mindset is so important. In so doing I will employ the following line of reasoning: 1. I will first discuss in more depth the need to persevere in one's faith. A hopeful mindset is essential to this perseverance. 2. I will follow this by demonstrating from Scripture that it is difficult to be saved. Many churches teach 'easy believism.' In other words, they teach that if you say the magic words, you are guaranteed entry into heaven. Nothing could be farther from the truth. 3. I will next demonstrate that some believers will have to endure what the Bible calls the 'Great Tribulation,' a final horrific period on Earth before the return of Jesus. During this period, belief in Jesus will be punishable by death. An assurance mindset could lead some to renounce faith in Jesus to save their lives thinking their salvation is assured. 4. I will follow this with a recap of the dangers of 'assurance teaching.' 5. Finally, I will point out the benefits of a 'hopeful' mindset. The Bible teaches there are benefits for having a 'hopeful' mindset both now and for eternity.

The Need for Perseverance

Probably the number one reason that a hopeful mindset is so important is that **it motivates a person to persevere in remaining faithful to the word of God**. A person with a hopeful mindset knows that his or her salvation is contingent on remaining faithful, so they will persevere in times when it is difficult to remain faithful. They may be tempted to take an easy path that is contrary to the word of God, but they know they might put their salvation in jeopardy. Therefore, they will be more inclined to take the difficult path of obedience. Let's look at some passages that confirm our need to persevere.

> 1 Timothy 4:16 "Pay close attention to yourself and to your teaching; **persevere in these things**; for **as you do this you will insure salvation both for yourself and for those who hear you**."
>
> James 1:12 "Blessed is a man who **perseveres** under trial; for **once he has been approved, he will receive the crown of life,** which the Lord has promised to those who love Him."
>
> Matthew 10:22 "And you will be hated by all on account of My name; but **it is the one who has endured to the end who will be saved**."

There are many more passages that confirm our need to persevere, but I think you get the picture. We indeed need to persevere in our faith until we die to gain salvation, and it will not be easy. In fact it is difficult to be saved. In the next section we will discuss the difficulties in gaining salvation.

It is Difficult to be Saved

I don't believe that churches today teach that it is difficult to be saved. On the contrary, with an assurance mindset, all one needs to do is sincerely repent of sins, profess belief in Jesus and proclaim that they will make Jesus Lord of their lives. The rest will work itself out. Jesus will complete our transformation, and we are just along for the ride. After all, the churches teach, we cannot contribute anything to our salvation.

I don't know about you, but I think persevering in difficult times takes effort on my part. It also involves a decision on my part. **We do have a part to play in the scheme of things, and we had better play it.** Let's look at a passage that confirms that it is difficult to be saved.

> 1 Peter 4:18 "And if **it is with difficulty that the righteous is saved**, what will become of the Godless man and the sinner?"

There it is, right from the mouth of the apostle Peter. It is difficult to be saved. If we didn't have any part in our own salvation, where would the difficulty be? I'm sure there are explanations from the assurance camp that reconcile this passage with 'assurance theology,' but it seems clear to me. It is difficult to remain on the pathway that leads to salvation. This next passage confirms the diligence required of us.

> Philippians 2:12-13 "...**work out your salvation with fear and trembling**; for it is God who is at work in you, both to will and to work for His good pleasure."

If we didn't have a part to play in our salvation, how could one explain this passage? This verse clearly refers to the believer's need to exert effort in keeping the faith. It even uses the 'work' word. The apostle Paul also confirmed the need to remain diligent by the following passage.

> 1 Corinthians 9:27 "...I buffet my body and make it my slave, lest possibly, after I have preached to others, I myself should be **disqualified**."

Paul knew that his salvation was not assured. He remained hopeful for his salvation and active in striving to obey the Word of God. Paul knew that the road to salvation was not easy, and the door to salvation was not thrown open to the masses. Jesus also confirmed the difficulty in gaining salvation in the following parallel verses.

> Luke 13:23-24 "And someone said to Him, "Lord, are there just a few who are being saved?" And He said to them, "Strive to enter by the narrow door; for **many, I tell you will seek to enter and will not be able**.""

> Matthew 7:13-14 "Enter by the narrow gate; for the gate is wide, and the way is broad that leads to destruction, and many are those who enter by it. **For**

the gate is small, and the way is narrow that leads to life, and <u>few</u> are those who find it."

If gaining salvation is easy, as some churches teach, Jesus' statements would not make sense. Many people have 'accepted Christ' in church. By their profession of faith, one could say they are 'seeking to enter.' But Jesus said that 'many will seek to enter but not be able.' Why are they not able? I believe they are not able to enter, because after their profession of faith they do not remain faithful to the Word of God. They do not 'work out their salvation with fear and trembling.'

There is another reason why having a 'hopeful mindset' is important, especially now. The Bible speaks of a time that precedes the return of Jesus to this earth. This time is called the Great Tribulation. A 'hopeful mindset' will be vitally important during that period.

The Great Tribulation

Perhaps the primary reason I am writing this book is that I believe the return of Jesus is not far off. It could conceivably happen in yours and my lifetime. I know that many past generations have felt this way, but the prerequisites for the 'end times' haven't been met until now. For example, the book of Revelation speaks of not being able to buy or sell anything unless one has the 'mark of the beast' on one's hand or forehead (Rev 13:17). To have that kind of financial control would require a cashless society with computer chip implants. The technology required for that hasn't existed until just recently.

The book of Revelation also speaks of the revival of the Roman Empire just prior to Jesus' return. The boundary of the recently formed European Community is virtually identical to the boundary of the ancient Roman Empire. We see the European Community gaining more and more unity with common currency, removal of border checkpoints and the common use of the English language in air traffic control. Complete unification is not far off.

The Bible speaks of a horrible time spanning three and one-half years just prior to Jesus' return. This period is called the Great Tribulation. During this time a dynamic person who the Bible calls 'the beast' will lead the resurrected Roman Empire. He will control all commerce and demand people worship him instead of God. Those who refuse will be put to death. It will be much like when the early church was persecuted by the Roman Emperor Nero. Those who professed belief and allegiance to Jesus Christ were put to death. This will happen again. Let's look at some passages that speak of this terrible time.

> Matthew 24:9-13 **"Then they will deliver you to tribulation, and will kill you, and you will be hated by all nations on account of My name.** And at that time many will fall away and will deliver up one another and hate one another. And many false prophets will arise, and will mislead many. And because lawlessness is increased, most people's love will grow cold. But the one who endures to the end, he shall be saved."
>
> Luke 21:16-19 **"But you will be delivered up even by parents and brothers and relatives and friends, and they will put some of you to death, and you will be hated by all on account of My name.** Yet not a hair of your head will perish. By your endurance you will gain your lives."

> Matthew 24:21-22 "**...for then there will be a great tribulation, such as has not occurred since the beginning of the world until now, nor ever shall.** And unless those days had been cut short, no life would have been saved; but for the sake of the elect those days shall be cut short."

Those who truly believe in and follow Jesus during the Great Tribulation will be 'enemies of the state.' They will be faced with the ultimate test of their faith in Jesus. Their very lives will be at stake. If they remain faithful to Jesus, they will be killed. However the Bible is very clear. If they renounce their faith in Jesus by taking the 'mark of the beast,' they will not gain salvation. They will spend an eternity in hell. Look at the following passage.

> Revelation 14:9-12 "**If anyone worships the beast and his image, and receives a mark on his forehead or upon his hand, he also will drink of the wine of the wrath of God,** which is mixed in full strength in the cup of His anger; and he will be tormented with fire and brimstone in the presence of the holy angels and in the presence of the Lamb. **And the smoke of their torment goes up <u>forever and ever</u>**; and they have no rest day and night, those who worship the beast and his image, and whoever receives the mark of his name. **Here is the perseverance of the saints who keep the commandments of God and their faith in Jesus.**"

What a horrible decision to have to face. Who will be prepared for such a test of faith? Are today's churches preparing their members for this difficult time? I don't think so. In fact, I believe many churches are unwittingly leading their members to destruction. First of all they are teaching that the church will not have to endure the Great Tribulation. They teach that there will be a 'rapture' of the church: a phenomenon where believers are removed from the world prior to the Great Tribulation. **This highly debatable position combined with the 'assurance mindset' leaves their congregations ill-prepared to face the ultimate test of their faith.**

Imagine the following scenario: You are a believer. You find yourself in a world where it is punishable by death to proclaim belief in Jesus Christ. You and your family are arrested and charged with believing in Jesus and for not allowing a computer chip to be implanted in your hand or forehead. You are told that charges against you and your family will be dropped if you renounce your faith in Jesus and receive the computer implant. However if you cling to your faith, you and your family will be killed. You are further advised that you will have to watch your children's execution before you are put to death. What will you do? I believe **your response to the situation will depend on whether you have a 'hopeful' or 'assurance' mindset.**

Let's assume for the moment you have the 'assurance' mindset. Your thought process may go something like this. 'I have been taught that I my salvation is assured because of my original conversion to Christianity. I have been taught that I cannot lose my salvation no matter what happens in my life. I have been taught that nothing can separate me from the love of God, not even my own choices. I will therefore tell these people what they want to hear and save my family. I will even submit myself to the new world order by taking a computer implant in my hand, so that I can buy the things my family needs. God will understand. He won't condemn me for trying to save my family.' The Bible says that this course of action will lead you to condemnation and loss of salvation. According to the Bible you will spend eternity in hell.

Now, let's assume that you have a 'hopeful' mindset. Your thought process may go something like this. 'The Bible teaches that I must not renounce my faith. I must not take the 'mark of the beast.' My very salvation is at stake depending on what I decide to do. If I want to have any hope of salvation, **I must be true to the Word of God, no matter what happens to me or to my family**. I will therefore pray to God to help me through this horrible ordeal and tell the authorities that I will not deny my faith in Jesus Christ or take the computer implant. My family and I will be executed.' The Bible says that by this course of action you will gain salvation. Your momentary pain will be replaced by an eternity of joy in heaven.

A 'hopeful' mindset will be absolutely essential during the Great Tribulation. And don't be fooled. The church will not be 'raptured' prior to those difficult times. The book of Revelation speaks of the Saints being killed by 'the beast.' It also speaks of the elect being subjected to the tribulation. If the church is gone, why are the elect still around to be persecuted? Look again at the following passage.

> Matthew 24:21-22 "...for then there will be a great tribulation, such as has not occurred since the beginning of the world until now, nor ever shall. **And unless those days had been cut short, no life would have been saved; but for the sake of the elect those days shall be cut short.**"

By now you should see that a 'hopeful' mindset is essential to surviving the Great Tribulation period. This mindset is not gained in a short period of time. It must be cultivated. 'Assurance teaching' prevents this from happening. In the next section I will further discuss the dangers of 'assurance teaching.'

More Dangers of Assurance Teaching

I believe that 'assurance teaching' produces believers that are too presumptive. In other words 'assurance teaching' produces believers that take their salvation for granted. This is not a good thing. Look at what the Bible says about presumption.

> Proverbs 13:10 "Through presumption comes nothing but strife, but with those who receive counsel is wisdom."
>
> Psalm 19:12-14 "Who can discern his errors? Acquit me of hidden faults. Also keep back Thy servant from presumptuous sins. Let them not rule over me. Then I shall be blameless, and I shall be acquitted of great transgression. Let the words of my mouth and the meditation of my heart be acceptable in Thy sight..."

At the risk of being branded a heretic, I would classify the 'assurance mindset' as a presumptive sin. It is a sin because this mindset is contrary to the Word of God. The notion that one's salvation is assured, no matter what, directly contradicts many Bible verses. Let me give you a few examples.

> Ezekiel 18:24 "But when a righteous man turns away from his righteousness, commits iniquity, and does according to all the abominations that a wicked man does, will he live? **All his righteous deeds which he has done will not be remembered for his treachery which he has committed and his sin which he has committed; for them he will die.**"
>
> 2 Peter 2:20-21 "For if after they have escaped the defilements of the world by the knowledge of the Lord and Savior Jesus Christ, they are again entangled in them and are overcome, the last state has become worse for them than the first. For **it would be better for them not to have known the way of righteousness, than having known it, to turn away from the holy commandment delivered to them.**"
>
> 2 Peter 3:17-18 "…be on your guard lest, being carried away by the error of unprincipled men, **you fall from your own steadfastness,** but grow in the grace and knowledge of our Lord and Savior Jesus Christ. To Him be the glory, both now and to the day of eternity. Amen."

There are many, many more passages like these; but these should demonstrate that one should not take one's salvation for granted. As I said before, even the apostle Paul was not presumptuous with regard to his salvation. Let's revisit what Paul said to the church at Philippi.

> Philippians 3:11-14 "…in order that I may attain to the resurrection from the dead. **Not that I have already obtained it, or have already become perfect, but I press on in order that I may lay hold**

of that for which also I was laid hold of by Christ Jesus. Brethren, <u>I do not regard myself as having laid hold of it yet</u>; but one thing I do: forgetting what lies behind and reaching forward to what lies ahead, I press on toward the goal for the prize of the upward call of God in Christ Jesus."

Paul continually cautioned the churches not to take their salvation for granted. He told them to nurture and to protect their faith in Jesus. He also told believers to evaluate themselves with regard to their faith as indicated in this passage.

> 2 Corinthians 13:5 "Test yourselves to see if you are in the faith; examine yourselves!"

Paul taught believers to fight against presumption. He certainly did not encourage them to take their salvation for granted. Look at these next verses.

> 1 Corinthians 10:12 "Therefore **let him who thinks he stands take heed lest he fall.**"
>
> Romans 11:19-22 "You will say then, "Branches were broken off so that I might be grafted in." Quite right, they were broken off for their unbelief, but you stand by your faith. **Do not be conceited but fear; for if God did not spare the natural branches, neither will He spare you.** Behold then the kindness and severity of God; to those who fell, severity, but to you, God's kindness, **<u>if</u> you continue in His kindness; otherwise you will be cut off.**"

Another reason the 'assurance teaching' is dangerous is that it doesn't help believers prepare for the daily tests of their faith. The Bible teaches that our faith in Jesus will be tested, whether we are new or seasoned believers. It seems that God is continually checking to see that our faith remains and is genuine. As with any test, it is possible to pass. It is also possible to fail. 'Assurance teaching' seems to minimize the importance of passing tests of faith. 'Assurance teachers' say that we may fail many tests of faith, but like the 'prodigal son,' we will return to God. 'Assurance teachers' say that we may fall away for a time, becoming 'carnal Christians,' but God will bring us back after a while. The only danger we may face is losing some rewards in heaven, but we will still go to heaven. This teaching is dangerous because it is false. It is contrary to the Word of God.

Those who continually fail their tests of faith do not become 'carnal Christians.' I believe they are more accurately characterized as unbelievers, and their salvation is not assured. Quite the contrary, continually failing their tests of faith will lead them to an eternity in hell. Let's look at what the Bible says.

> John 15:1-2 "I am the true vine, and my Father is the vinedresser. **Every branch in Me that does not bear fruit, He takes away;** and every branch that bears fruit, He prunes it, that it may bear more fruit."
>
> Psalm 11:5 "**The Lord tests the righteous and the wicked...**"
>
> Proverbs 19:16 "He who keeps the commandment keeps his soul, but **he who is careless of his ways will die.**"

These passages make it clear that our decisions during times of testing are crucial to our eternal destination. Yes, we will fail from time to time. But our response to our failures is also important. Do our failures make us truly sorry and truly determined to not fail again? Or do our failures merely give us something to mention half-heartedly the next time we are in church? I believe 'assurance teaching' yields the latter response.

True repentance and change only happens with major effort in our lives. **If we think we don't have to do it (change), we won't.** 'Assurance teaching' leads us to believe that repentance is not important to our eternal destination. It teaches that we might experience hardships because of our decisions, but we will still make it to heaven. This leads many to keep their sins, which they enjoy, thinking they will only have consequences during their lives on earth. That, they reason, is OK, as long as they make it into heaven. According to the Bible, that mindset will lead them directly to hell.

The Benefits of a Hopeful Mindset

While it is true that the 'assurance' mindset is dangerous to our eternal destination, it is also true that a 'hopeful' mindset gives us greater security for our salvation. A 'hopeful' mindset also has tangible benefits during our lives here on earth. A 'hopeful' mindset leads one to place more trust in the Lord, and this trust yields benefits. Let's look at what the Bible says.

> Jeremiah 17:7-8 "**Blessed is the man who trusts in the Lord and whose trust is the Lord.** For he will be like a tree planted by the water, that extends its roots by a stream and will not fear when the heat comes; but its leaves will be green, and it will not be anxious in a year of drought nor cease to yield fruit."

> Isaiah 26:2-3 "... **the one that <u>remains</u> faithful. The <u>steadfast of mind</u> Thou wilt keep in perfect peace, because he trusts in Thee.**"

As these passages indicate, trusting the Lord makes one more effective for the Lord. It also keeps one from being anxious or fearful during the tough times. When one trusts the Lord, he or she knows that the Lord is in control of everything, and that person is OK with what the Lord has in mind for them. Here's another passage.

> Psalm 32:10-11 "Many are the sorrows of the wicked; but **he who trusts in the Lord, lovingkindness shall surround him**. Be glad in the Lord and rejoice, you righteous ones, and shout for joy, all you who are upright in heart."

This verse indicates that the Lord will bless those who trust in Him. It also implies that those who don't trust in the Lord are classified as wicked and have many hardships. God considers those who trust in Him to be righteous and upright in heart. Let's look at another well-known passage.

> Proverbs 3:5-6 "**Trust in the Lord with all your heart, and do not lean on your own understanding. In all your ways acknowledge Him, and He will make your paths straight.**"

If you trust in the Lord, He will keep you on the right path- the path to salvation. As you may have discovered, life throws you many 'curve balls,' and you must be prepared to handle them. A life characterized by trusting the Lord, believing in the Word of God and doing what it tells us to do, will enable us to respond correctly to the challenges that life gives us.

As Psalm 32 indicates, God considers those who trust in Him to be righteous and upright in heart. The Bible has much to say about the benefits of being considered righteous by the Lord. Here are some of those passages.

> 1 Peter 3:12 "For the eyes of the Lord are upon the righteous, and **His ears attend to their prayer…**"
>
> Psalm 92:12-14 "The righteous man will flourish like the palm tree. He will grow like a cedar in Lebanon. Planted in the house of the Lord, they will flourish in the courts of our God. **They will still yield fruit in old age.** They shall be full of sap and very green…"
>
> James 5:16 "The effective prayer of a righteous man can accomplish much."

These are very intriguing passages, because they infer that God may not listen to all prayers. I have heard many people say they will pray for this or that, but will God listen to and respond to their prayers? Perhaps. I really don't know. However **one sure way to get God's attention is to trust in Him and live your life accordingly**. When God considers you righteous, He hears your prayers and acts on them. More significantly, when you trust in the Lord and align your heart with His, the desires of your heart will be granted to you. The Bible says that very clearly in the following passage.

> Psalm 37:4 "Delight yourself in the Lord; and He will give you the desires of your heart."

I remember reading this passage years ago and thinking, 'gee, if the desires of my heart are to be wealthy, the Lord will make it so.' Unfortunately, I wasn't focusing on the first part of the passage. If I truly 'delight myself in the Lord,' I will be 'transformed by the renewing of my mind;' and then the desires of my heart will be for the things the Lord wants me to possess.

Let's look at a few more passages that speak to the benefits of being considered righteous by the Lord.

> Proverbs 13:21 "Adversity pursues sinners, but the righteous will be rewarded with prosperity."
>
> Psalm 34:19 "Many are the afflictions of the righteous; but the Lord delivers him out of them all."
>
> Proverbs 12:21 "No harm befalls the righteous, but the wicked are filled with trouble."
>
> Proverbs 10:24 "What the wicked fears will come upon him, and the desire of the righteous will be granted."

The Bible is quite clear. Those who are considered righteous by the Lord lead lives that are far superior to the rest. They may have challenges, but the challenges do not create excessive anxiety or fear. In fact, those who really trust the Lord are actually at peace during those difficult times because they know God is in control and will work things out.

The Bible also characterizes those who have a 'hopeful' mindset as those who 'fear the Lord.' This is a healthy fear, a fear that keeps one on the right track. Those who really believe the Word of God know the power of God. They know He can keep us alive or not. More importantly they know He has the power to send us to heaven or hell. Here is a passage that links 'fearing the Lord' to a 'hopeful' mindset.

Psalm 33:18-19 "Behold, the eye of the Lord is on **those who fear Him, on those who hope for His loving-kindness,** to deliver their soul from death…"

At this point it would be productive to discuss what it means to 'fear the Lord.' There are some who look on fear in general as a bad thing. A friend of mine recently said he believes that fear is the result of ignorance. Fear, he believes, will be erased by education or by understanding. Can his reasoning be applied to fearing God? If we become 'educated' will the need to fear God be erased? I don't think so. Let me explain.

Fearing God is the same as respecting God. When we were children we feared our fathers. Why? Because we dreaded the punishment he would deliver if we didn't obey him. We showed our fathers great respect for that reason. We should fear or respect God for the same reason. He is our heavenly Father, and He is capable of delivering significant punishment if we don't obey Him. This fear will not and should not be eradicated by education. Avoiding punishment is a logical and smart thing to do.

The Bible says, "The fear of the Lord is the beginning of wisdom…" (Psalm 111:10) Fear gives us an initial motivation to obey God. We will then find that this obedience brought on by our healthy fear will lead to very good things in our lives. Let's look at some of the benefits of fearing God.

Psalm 112

:1 "How blessed is the man who fears the Lord, who greatly delights in His commandments.

:2 His descendants will be mighty on earth…

:3 Wealth and riches are in his house…

:5 He will maintain his cause in judgment.

:6 For he will never be shaken…

:7 He will not fear evil tidings; his heart is steadfast, trusting in the Lord.

:8 His heart is upheld, he will not fear…"

Psalm 128:1-4 "How blessed is everyone who fears the Lord, who walks in His ways. When you shall eat of the fruit of your hands, you will be happy and it will be well with you. Your wife shall be like a fruitful vine within your house, your children like olive plants around your table. Behold, for thus shall the man be blessed who fears the Lord."

Psalm 147:11 "The Lord favors those who fear Him, those who wait for His loving-kindness."

Psalm 25:12-14 "Who is the man who fears the Lord? He will instruct him in the way he should choose. His soul will abide in prosperity, and his descendants will inherit the land. The secret of the Lord is for those who fear Him, and He will make them know His covenant."

Psalm 34:7 "The angel of the Lord encamps around those who fear Him, and rescues them."

Psalm 34:9 "O fear the Lord, you His saints; for those who fear Him there is no want."

At this point you should understand the importance of having a 'hopeful' versus 'assurance' mindset when it comes to your eternal destiny. You should also understand why one cannot know for certain that he or she is of God's elect. The best one can do is to live a life characterized by faith in God's Word and hope for salvation. In the next section I will attempt to convey Biblical instruction regarding our daily lives. After learning these important truths, how do we best apply them in our lives or 'how then should we live?'

Section IV

HOW THEN SHALL WE LIVE

At this point you may be wondering, 'what kind of a life will keep me on the pathway to salvation?' To state it another way, 'how then should we live?' I touched briefly on this already, but it would be beneficial to look in more depth. I don't think it is possible to address all situations we may encounter in our lives, but I think we can develop habit patterns and strategies that will tend to keep us on the pathway to salvation and 'make our hope sure.'

The Bible teaches that the kind of life that will lead to salvation is one that is characterized by faith, faith in the Word of God, faith in Jesus Christ. Good so far; but how exactly does that faith play itself out in one's life? What does it look like? First of all, I believe that 'saving faith' is something that needs to be nourished and refreshed daily. The best way to do that is to read the Bible daily.

As you may know there are many Bibles from which to choose. Also, some are organized in easy to read formats that make daily reading more structured. I personally read a Bible called the 'One Year Bible,' which is separated into daily readings from both the Old and New Testaments. This is a great format that requires about thirty minutes to one hour of your time each day. I prefer the New American Standard Bible (NASB) version, believing that it is an accurate word for word translation of the original Biblical languages: Hebrew, Aramaic and Greek. There are other versions of the 'One Year Bible.' I believe the New International Version (NIV) and the New King James Version (NKJV) are also good translations.

Set aside a time of the day when you are most alert and can be alone and undisturbed. My time is very early in the morning before the rest of the household is awake. Before beginning to read, pray to God for help in understanding what you are about to read and how to apply it. It also is crucial that you believe what you are about to read is absolutely the truth.

Daily Bible reading does several things for you. First of all it recharges your faith. Secondly, it puts you in the proper frame of mind to face the daily challenges that will come your way. Thirdly, it has the effect of 'renewing your mind' and keeping you from conforming to the sinful world in which you live. Finally, it gives you specific directions on how to live.

Let's discuss some strategies, decisions and habit patterns that are beneficial and necessary for 'right living' and for dealing with the inevitable tests of our faith. First of all, we must have and cultivate a mindset by which we commit ourselves to live by faith in the Word of God. We must also be willing to take risks as we exercise our faith. In other words we sometimes need to make decisions without seeing the benefits. For example, the Bible tells us, "Let each one do just as he has purposed in his heart; not grudgingly or under compulsion; for God loves a cheerful giver." (2 Corinthians 9:7) We are called to be generous and cheerful in our giving. Therefore we should do so, even though we don't see any tangible benefits other than knowing God will bless us by our actions. That is 'living by faith.' However the real driver of genuine faith is to believe that God is in control of everything.

Nothing happens in this universe without God causing it or allowing it to happen. Some people don't believe that God gets involved with the small things, but look at the following passages from Psalm 139:

> Psalm 139:1-4 "O Lord, Thou hast searched me and known me. Thou dost know when I sit down and when I rise up; Thou dost understand my thought from afar. Thou dost scrutinize my path and my lying down, and art intimately acquainted with all my ways. **Even before there is a word on my tongue, behold, O Lord, Thou dost know it all."**

> Psalm 139:13-16 "For Thou didst form my inward parts; Thou didst weave me in my mother's womb. I will give thanks to Thee, for I am fearfully and wonderfully made; Wonderful are Thy works, and my soul knows it very well. My frame was not hidden from Thee, when I was made in secret, and skillfully wrought in the depths of the earth. Thine eyes have seen my unformed substance; and **in Thy book they were all written, the days that were ordained for me, when as yet there was not one of them."**

God knows our thoughts and our words before we do. That's amazing. He knows everything. He created each and every one of us. He knows how we will live, and He knows how and when each of us will die. I don't know about you, but **that knowledge gives me freedom to live my life without fear, because I don't control my destiny. God does.** I am free to live; free to live a life of faith in the Word of God.

So then, what should be the framework within which we live our lives of faith in the Word of God? Jesus gives us this framework in the following passage:

> Mark 12:28-31 "What commandment is the foremost of all?" Jesus answered, "The foremost is, 'Hear O Israel! The Lord our God is one Lord; and you shall love the Lord your God with all your heart, and with all your soul, and with all your mind, and with all your strength.' The second is this, 'You shall love your neighbor as yourself.' There is no other commandment greater than these.'"

We should live our lives in such a way that we do what Jesus tells us to do. After all, the requirement for salvation is to believe in Jesus. Right? If we really believe in Him, we will take Him seriously and do what He says. Jesus tells us first to Love God. What does that mean? The following passages give us guidance in this important matter.

> 2 John 1:6 "And this is love, that we walk according to His commandments."
>
> John 14:15 "**If you love Me, you will keep My commandments.**"
>
> John 14:21 "**He who has My commandments and keeps them, he it is who loves Me**; and he who loves Me shall be loved by My Father, and I will love him, and will disclose Myself to him."

John 14:23 "Jesus answered and said to him, "**If anyone loves Me, he will keep My word**; and My Father will love him, and We will come to him, and make Our abode with him.""

So then, loving God is not just a warm fuzzy feeling. **Loving God is evidenced by actually doing what He tells us to do.** If we say we love God and don't obey Him, we are liars. We don't love Him. What then does God command of us? Where do we look? You guessed it. The Bible has all the answers. Here are just a few of His commands.

Ephesians 4:22-24 "…in reference to your former manner of life, you **lay aside the old self, which is being corrupted in accordance with the lusts of deceit**, and that you be renewed in the spirit of your mind, and put on the new self, which in the likeness of God has been created in righteousness and holiness of the truth."

Romans 13:11-14 "And this do, knowing the time, that it is already the hour for you to awaken from sleep; for now salvation is nearer to us than when we believed. The night is almost gone, and the day is at hand. Let us therefore lay aside the deeds of darkness and put on the armor of light. **Let us behave properly as in the day, not in carousing and drunkenness, not in sexual promiscuity and sensuality, not in strife and jealousy.** But put on the Lord Jesus Christ, and make no provision for the flesh in regard to its lusts."

Psalm 34:13-14 "Keep your tongue from evil, and your lips from speaking deceit. Depart from evil and do good; seek peace and pursue it."

We see from these passages that we need to strive diligently to move away from a sinful way of life. In short, we need to stop sinning and lead clean lives. The Bible makes it pretty clear by various passages the behaviors we are to avoid. As I previously mentioned, some behaviors are easy to avoid. Some are not. Those are the ones that demand our best efforts. However if we diligently strive not to sin, God will help us in those efforts, and we will be demonstrating our love for God.

In addition to loving God, we are also called to 'love our neighbor as ourselves.' With this commandment, we must answer two questions: 1.) Who are our neighbors? 2.) How do we love them? First of all, I believe our 'neighbor' is a person or persons that God brings into our lives. It might be our physical neighbor. It might be somebody at work or somebody in our church. It might be a family member. It might be the beggar on the street. It might be a family in need that comes to our mind. **Whoever it is, we will know at our deepest level that they have been placed in our lives.** Our love for them is evidenced by action on our part, and the Bible gives us specific instructions regarding what we are to do. Let's look at some passages.

> 1 John 3:17-18 "**…whoever has the world's goods, and beholds his brother in need and closes his heart against him, how does the love of God abide in him?** Little children, let us not love with word or with tongue, but in deed and truth."

> Philippians 2:3-4 "Do nothing from selfishness or empty conceit, but with humility of mind **let each of you regard one another as more important than himself; do not merely look out for your own personal interests, but also for the interests of others.**"

> 1 Thessalonians 5:13-15 "Live in peace with one another. And we urge you, brethren, admonish the unruly, encourage the fainthearted, help the weak, be patient with all men. See that no one repays another with evil for evil, but always seek after that which is good for one another and for all men."

From these passages we see that we are sometimes called to help others. We are not to live isolated lives. We are sometimes called to give our time, sometimes our talents and sometimes our 'treasures.' Sometimes we are called to give all three. I believe that God will speak to us with a quiet voice that urges us to help certain people. Listen to that voice. By helping we are demonstrating our love for others. We are also demonstrating our love for God. Look at the following passage by which Peter gives us a pattern for our lives.

> 2 Peter 1:5-8 "Now for this very reason also, applying all diligence, in your faith supply moral excellence, and in your moral excellence, knowledge; and in your knowledge, self-control, and in your self-control, perseverance, and in your perseverance, godliness; and in your godliness, brotherly kindness, and in your brotherly kindness, love. For if these qualities are yours and are increasing, they render you neither useless nor unfruitful in the true knowledge of our Lord Jesus Christ."

By this passage we again see that the journey to salvation is a process. It is a process by which we are gradually transformed from our natural sinful selves into people characterized by faith in the Word of God. We are transformed into people who demonstrate their love for God and their love for their 'neighbors.' It is a process, and at times this process is not easy.

To be honest, the process of being transformed is difficult. It is difficult because it requires us to struggle against what we naturally desire. The apostle Paul characterized it as the struggle of the 'spirit' against the 'flesh.' The 'spirit' is the part of us that wants to obey God. The 'flesh' is the part of us that wants to sin. It is a struggle that Paul knew all too well. Like us, he faced it on a daily basis. Let's look at what Paul said in this regard.

> Romans 7:18-19 "For I know that nothing good dwells in me, that is, in my flesh; for the wishing is present in me, but the doing of the good is not. For the good that I wish, I do not do; but I practice the very evil that I do not wish."

Wow! Even the Apostle Paul had trouble fighting sin in his life; and he had a close personal relationship with Jesus Christ. You might think, 'what's the use in my trying to fight sin if the apostle Paul had trouble?' There is great benefit in continuing to struggle against sin, and we must never give up the struggle. **In fact, I believe that it is precisely in the struggle that we are being saved.** Look at the following passage.

> Romans 8:5-8 "For those who are according to the flesh set their minds on the things of the flesh, but those who are according to the Spirit, the things of the Spirit. For the mind set on the flesh is death, but the mind set on the Spirit is life and peace, because the mind set on the flesh is hostile toward God; for it does not subject itself to the law of God, for it is not even able to do so; and those who are in the flesh cannot please God."

By this passage we see that it is vitally important where we set our minds. If we daily set our minds on being obedient to God, we are setting our minds on the Spirit. Our desire is not to sin; and even though we may occasionally sin, we are not content with it. The sin doesn't characterize us because it is something we didn't want to do. On the other hand if we set our minds on the flesh, we will indeed sin, and the sin will characterize us. We will be in bondage to it, and the outcome will be spiritual death. I don't think that we want to be spiritually dead when we physically die. I shudder at the probable consequences.

So then, we must continually struggle against the desire to sin for the rest of our lives. The good news is that the Bible gives us strategies and motivates us to continue the fight. Look at what Jesus told his followers.

> Mark 8:34-36 "And He summoned the multitudes with His disciples and said to them, "If anyone wishes to come after Me, let him deny himself, and take up his cross and follow Me. For whoever wishes to save his life shall lose it; but whoever loses his life for My sake and the gospel's shall save it. For what does it profit a man to gain the whole world, and forfeit his soul?""

Jesus motivates us with His words. He is saying that if you give up a sinful life you will receive real life. God is not a 'cosmic killjoy.' The life of a believer is not boring and/or sad with nothing enjoyable. Rather it is rich, full and exciting. However to experience it one must take a risk and truly give up the momentary pleasures of sin. Let's look at another motivational passage.

> 1 John 2:15-17 "Do not love the world, nor the things in the world. **If anyone loves the world, the love of the Father is not in him.** For all that is in the world, the lust of the flesh and the lust of the eyes and the boastful pride of life, is not from the Father, but is from the world. And the world is passing away, and also its lusts; **but the one who does the will of God abides forever.**"

This passage tells us that we must turn away from the sinful things of the world in order to gain salvation. It tells us that loving sinful things and loving God are mutually exclusive. You can't successfully do both, though many try. Let's look at the following strategy for turning away from sin.

> Galatians 5:16-17 "But I say, **walk by the Spirit, and you will not carry out the desire of the flesh.** For the flesh sets its desire against the Spirit, and the Spirit against the flesh; for these are in opposition to one another…"

This passage tells us to 'walk by the Spirit.' What does that mean? If we walk by the Spirit of God we will be seeking always to please Him by doing what He wants us to do. And as we do this, we will be given what the Bible calls the fruits of the Spirit, which are '…love, joy, peace, patience, kindness, goodness, faithfulness, gentleness and self-control…' (Galatians 5:22-23) As these traits grow within us, they will begin to characterize us; and we will be better able to turn away from sin in our lives. Let's look at another effective strategy for avoiding sin.

> Philippians 4:8 "Finally, brethren, whatever is true, whatever is honorable, whatever is right, whatever is

pure, whatever is lovely, whatever is of good repute, if there is any excellence and if anything worthy of praise, let your mind dwell on these things."

As I have previously mentioned, our thought process is extremely important, because sin begins in our minds. Keeping our thoughts focused on good things will keep us from sinning. This takes conscious effort on our part because the mind is prone to wander. It is especially prone to wander to sinful thoughts. We are called to avoid thinking or dwelling on evil things. As the apostle Paul said to the church at Corinth, "Brethren, do not be children in your thinking; yet **in evil be babes, but in your thinking be mature.**" (1 Corinthians 14:20)

Let's next revisit probably the most important strategy for avoiding sin, putting on the 'full armor of God.'

> Ephesians 6:10-18 "Finally, be strong in the Lord, and in the strength of His might. **Put on the full armor of God, that you may be able to stand firm against the schemes of the devil.** For our struggle is not against flesh and blood, but against the rulers, against the powers, against the world forces of this darkness, against the spiritual forces of wickedness in the heavenly places. Therefore, **take up the full armor of God, that you may be able to resist in the evil day, and having done everything, to stand firm**. Stand firm therefore, having girded your loins with **truth**, and having put on the **breastplate of righteousness**, and having shod your feet with the **preparation of the gospel of peace**; in addition to all, taking up the **shield of faith** with which you will be able to extinguish all the flaming missiles of the evil one. And take the **helmet of salvation**, and

the **sword of the Spirit**, which is the word of God. With all prayer and petition pray at all times in the Spirit, and with this in view, **be on the alert with all perseverance…**"

In this passage Paul describes 'the armor of God.' These are spiritual implements that we must daily wear in order to resist temptation, avoid sin and stand against evil. Notice that two of the implements, the Truth and the Word of God, are the Bible. I can't overemphasize the importance of reading and studying the Bible on a daily basis. We must be firmly anchored in the truth in order to fight deception, which Satan uses so effectively to derail us. The other implements are important as well, and we should briefly look at each of them.

<u>Girding our loins with Truth.</u> We must literally clothe ourselves with The Word of God, the Bible. It must surround us and protect us from the lies of the world. There is only one truth given to us in this world. Jesus Christ, who is The Truth, is the Living Word of God. The Living Word of God is given to us in a readable form, The Bible. We must study it daily.

<u>The Breastplate of Righteousness.</u> Simply put, the breastplate protects our vital organs, especially the heart. If it is pierced we will die. In a similar way, if we pursue a sinful life, we will die spiritually, though we may be physically alive. Therefore we must pursue right living in order to become and remain spiritually alive.

<u>Preparation of the Gospel of Peace.</u> The Gospel message presented in the Bible is the message about Jesus Christ, who is the only way to salvation. We must know this Gospel message and be able to communicate it to others. This requires study and preparation on our part.

The Shield of Faith. Satan will continue to try to derail us as we journey toward salvation. Our faith in Jesus Christ who is the living Word of God will strengthen us and keep us from becoming discouraged. It will also keep us from being deceived and moved away from the truth.

The Helmet of Salvation. This is our 'hope of salvation' to which we tenaciously cling as we live our daily lives. This hope protects another of our vital parts, the head. We must maintain this hope until we die, or our motivation to persevere in obeying God will disappear.

The Sword of the Spirit. This is the Word of God, the Bible. It is our only offensive implement in the 'full armor of God.' We are not called to merely be passive on our journey toward salvation. We are called to stand firm for 'the faith.' (Philippians 1:27) We are also called to expose evil. (Ephesians 5:11) However we cannot do this effectively without being firmly rooted in the Bible. We must know the truth so well, that when a lie appears we recognize it immediately. We are also called to expose that lie.

So, we see that we are to live lives that move us away from sinful things, and we are to cling tenaciously to Jesus Christ. We are to expect difficulties on our journey to salvation, but we are to be gradually transformed away from our sinful selves. I don't believe this transformation is abrupt. It is gradual, and we should recognize it as such. I don't think it is wise to force the transformation, as the following passage indicates.

> Ecclesiastes 7:16-17 "Do **not be excessively righteous and do not be overly wise**. Why should you ruin yourself? **Do not be excessively wicked and do not be a fool.** Why should you die before your time?"

By this passage King Solomon tells us that we shouldn't be excessively righteous. Really? Wouldn't that be good? When I first read this passage, I was taken aback. Then I thought about it while looking at my own life. I realized that I couldn't handle an abrupt and sweeping spiritual change in my life. For example, I couldn't shed my life with my family and career and immediately attend a seminary. It just wouldn't work. No. **I have to gradually become the person God wants me to be within the environment He has placed me.**

In this section I have hopefully provided some Biblical guidance on how we should live our lives as we journey toward salvation. There is indeed much more guidance in the Bible, and I leave it to you to discover the many gems that are provided in the Word of God. As you draw closer to God, He will draw closer to you, and your journey will be a wonderful adventure. As the Bible says, **"Trust in the Lord with all your heart, and <u>do not lean on your own understanding</u>. In all your ways acknowledge Him, and He will make your paths straight."** (Proverbs 3:5-6)

CONCLUSION

I BELIEVE THAT MOST OF us want to know what happens to us after we die. We also have a hope that we will continue to exist and to exist in a better state than we have here on earth. Many of us have been told from our youth that there is a God and that He created everything. We have also been taught that there is heaven and there is hell, and we will spend eternity in one of those places. If we are Christian, we have been taught that the requirement for admittance into heaven is to believe in Jesus Christ, the only Son of God. We have been taught that if we believe in Jesus we will go to heaven. However we have not really been taught what that belief means. Furthermore we have not really been taught to any real satisfaction, who Jesus is. I have attempted in this book to clarify the Biblical pathway to salvation.

To briefly recap, the pathway to salvation is exclusively through Jesus Christ. However we cannot successfully find or proceed down that path until we accurately characterize Jesus. The Bible provides the only way to know Jesus. We must read and study the Bible to know Jesus. Only then can we rightly believe in Him. The Bible also teaches that it is difficult to be saved. We will encounter many trials in our lives to test our faith, and we must persevere in our faith to gain salvation. The Bible does not teach that our salvation is assured. It does teach that we can and must maintain a healthy hope for our salvation. Hope helps us to persevere in being faithful to the Word of God and will keep us on that pathway to salvation. **Thinking our salvation is assured works against that necessary perseverance, and will in all likelihood keep us from salvation.**

In this book I have also defended the assertion that no one can know for certain that he or she is one of God's elect, predestined to gain salvation. One can, however, know if he or she has what the Bible calls 'eternal life.' **Eternal life has both a present and future value and is directly linked to an active belief in Jesus Christ.** Because we have freedom of choice, we always have the potential of departing from believing in and knowing Jesus. If we choose to turn away from Jesus, we will lose the life He provides. If we physically die in our unbelief, we will not gain salvation.

My hope is that this book has given you an understanding of what the Bible teaches regarding salvation. The Bible is our only sure anchor and source of truth in this important matter. Churches are not necessarily a reliable source of truth. In fact, many churches depart from the truth and lead people astray. **Each of us has the ability and the responsibility to seek the truth.** We also have a mandate to obey God's Word. As we diligently and favorably respond to the truth God gives us, He will give us more truth; and we will 'grow in the grace and knowledge of our Lord and Savior Jesus Christ.' (2 Peter 3:18) **If we persevere in** our faith and continue to grow in God's truth, God will 'make our hope sure.' (Hebrews 6:11) After our life here on earth is finished, Jesus will say to us 'well done good and faithful servant;' (Matthew 25:21) and we will 'dwell in the house of the Lord forever.' (Psalm 23:6)

www.ingramcontent.com/pod-product-compliance
Lightning Source LLC
Chambersburg PA
CBHW071455080526
44587CB00014B/2112